Alfred Perceval Graves

Irish Songs and Ballads

Alfred Perceval Graves

Irish Songs and Ballads

ISBN/EAN: 9783743306417

Manufactured in Europe, USA, Canada, Australia, Japa

Cover: Foto ©ninafisch / pixelio.de

Manufactured and distributed by brebook publishing software (www.brebook.com)

Alfred Perceval Graves

Irish Songs and Ballads

TABLE OF CONTENTS.

	PAGE
DEDICATION	v
PREFACE	ix
SONGS AND BALLADS	1
RUSTIC POEMS	69
ANGLO-IRISH BALLADS	105
FROM THE CELTIC	123
SONGS AND SKETCHES	153
MUSIC	201
MUSICAL NOTE	202
NOTES	241
INDEX	271

PREFACE.

MOST of the Songs and Ballads in this volume, if not actually composed to the music of old Irish airs, owe to them their prime impulse and complete character. I speak in the main of airs in Bunting's collection, which have been left untouched by Moore, and of others in Petrie's and Hoffmann's collections, published after the last of the poet's Irish melodies, which will therefore be fresh to all but specialists in Irish music. Whenever the Celtic or Anglo-Irish words to these airs or fragments of them remained, I have not for a moment scrupled to press into my service whatever appeared to me poetical in the original; though in such cases I have taken care in the notes at the end of this volume to give my readers an opportunity of comparing my version with these older forms.

Under this head will be found such songs of occupation as the Smith's Song, the Mill Song, and Spinning and Weaving Songs; Fishing, Hunting, and Farming Ballads; Convivial Songs to the Jig and Planxty, and a Festal Chorus; the Loobeen, or Irish Amœbæan; Love Songs and Love Ballads, Lullabies and Lamentations. In order that the reader may be able to realize the character of the more remarkable Irish airs to which my songs are written, seven and twenty of them are printed in a musical appendix to this volume.

Some half-dozen of these, arranged as songs by Mr. Joseph Robinson, have been published separately by Messrs. Cramer,

Wood, and Co., of Westmorland Street, Dublin, and it is probable that others will see the light shortly.

With regard to the poems of an Idyllic character in my book, I cannot do more than say that they are the outcome of an affectionate study of Irish peasant-life among the mountains of Kerry.

A few Bardic Lyrics are presented in verse closely translated from the Celtic, and a long poem, "The Fairy Branch," based upon a somewhat homely prose original, a reference to which will be found in the notes, is put forward as an experiment in the poetical treatment of early Irish tales.

I desire here to acknowledge my deep indebtedness to Dr. P. W. Joyce, the author of "Old Celtic Romances" and "Irish Names of Places," for the invaluable aid which, as a Celtic scholar, a literary critic, and a leading authority in Irish music and song, he has rendered me throughout the course of this work.

ALFRED PERCEVAL GRAVES,
20, Greenhead Road, Huddersfield.

May, 1880.

SONGS AND BALLADS.

THE LITTLE RED LARK.

Oh, swan of slenderness,
Dove of tenderness,
   Jewel of joys, arise!
The little red lark
Like a rosy spark
   Of song to his sunburst flies.
But till thou art risen
Earth is a prison
   Full of my lonesome sighs;
Then awake and discover
To thy fond lover
   The morn of thy matchless eyes.

The dawn is dark to me
Hark! oh, hark to me,
   Pulse of my heart, I pray!
And out of thy hiding
With blushes gliding,
   Dazzle me with thy day.

Ah, then, once more to thee
Flying I'll pour to thee
   Passion so sweet and gay,
The lark shall listen,
And dewdrops glisten,
   Laughing on every spray.

LOVE'S WISHES.

Would I were Erin's apple-blossom o'er you,
   Or Erin's rose in all its beauty blown,
To drop my richest petals down before you,
   Within the garden where you walk alone;
In hope you'd turn and pluck a little posy,
   With loving fingers through my foliage pressed,
And kiss it close and set it blushing rosy
   To sigh out all its sweetness on your breast.

Would I might take the pigeon's flight towards you,
   And perch beside your window-pane above,
And murmur how my heart of hearts it hoards you,
   O hundred thousand treasures of my love;
In hope you'd stretch your slender hand and take me,
   And smooth my wildly-fluttering wings to rest,
And lift me to your loving lips and make me
   My bower of blisses in your loving breast.

I ONCE LOVED A BOY.

I ONCE loved a boy, and a bold Irish boy,
    Far away in the hills of the West ;
Ah ! the love of that boy was my jewel of joy.
    And I built him a bower in my breast,
        In my breast ;
    And I built him a bower in my breast.

I once loved a boy, and I trusted him true,
    And I built him a bower in my breast ;
But away, wirrasthrue ! the rover he flew,
    And robbed my poor heart of its rest,
        Of its rest ;
    And robbed my poor heart of its rest.

The spring-time returns, and the sweet speckled thrush
    Murmurs soft to his mate on her nest,
But for ever there's fallen a sorrowful hush
    O'er the bower that I built in my breast,
        In my breast ;
    O'er the desolate bower in my breast.

THE BANKS OF THE DAISIES.

When first I saw young Molly
  Stretched beneath the holly,
Fast asleep, forenint her sheep, one dreamy summer's day,
  With daisies laughing round her,
  Hand and foot I bound her,
Then kissed her on her blooming cheek, and softly stole away.

  But, as with blushes burning
  Tip-toe I was turning,
From sleep she starts, and on me darts a dreadful lightning ray:
  My foolish flowery fetters
  Scornfully she scatters,
And like a winter sunbeam she coldly sweeps away.

  But Love, young Love, comes stooping
  O'er my daisies drooping,
And oh! each flower with fairy power the rosy boy renews:
  Then twines each charming cluster
  In links of starry lustre,
And with the chain enchanting my colleen proud pursues.

And soon I met young Molly
Musing melancholy,
With downcast eyes and starting sighs, along the meadow bank :
And oh ! her swelling bosom
Was wreathed with daisy blossom,
Like stars in summer heaven, as in my arms she sank.

HERRING IS KING.

Let all the fish that swim the sea,
    Salmon and turbot, cod and ling,
Bow down the head, and bend the knee
    To herring, their king! to herring, their king:
Sing, Hugamar féin an sowra lin',
'Tis we have brought the summer in.

The sun sank down so round and red
    Upon the bay, upon the bay;
The sails shook idle overhead,
    Becalmed we lay, becalmed we lay;
Sing, Hugamar féin an sowra lin',
'Tis we have brought the summer in.

Till Shawn the eagle dropped on deck
    The bright-eyed boy, the bright-eyed boy;
'Tis he has spied your silver track,
    Herring, our joy, herring, our joy;
Sing, Hugamar féin an sowra lin',
'Tis we have brought the summer in.

It was in with the sails and away to shore,
    With the rise and swing, the rise and swing
Of two stout lads at each smoking oar,
    After herring, our king, herring, our king :
Sing, Hugamar féin an sowra lin',
'Tis we have brought the summer in.

The Manx and the Cornish raised the shout,
    And joined the chase and joined the chase :
But their fleets they fouled as they went about,
    And we won the race, we won the race ;
Sing, Hugamar féin an sowra lin',
'Tis we have brought the summer in.

For we turned and faced you full to land,
    Down the góleen long, the góleen long,
And, after you, slipped from strand to strand
    Our nets so strong, our nets so strong ;
Sing, Hugamar féin an sowra lin',
'Tis we have brought the summer in.

Then we called to our sweethearts and our wives,
    "Come welcome us home, welcome us home,"
Till they ran to meet us for their lives
    Into the foam, into the foam ;

Sing, Hugamar féin an sowra lin',
'Tis we have brought the summer in.

O the kissing of hands and waving of caps
   From girl and boy, from girl and boy,
While you leapt by scores in the lasses' laps.
   Herring, our joy, herring, our joy :
Sing, Hugamar féin an sowra lin',
'Tis we have brought the summer in.

HUSH SONG.

I would hush my lovely laddo,
In the green arbutus' shadow,
O'er the fragrant, flowering meadow,
    In the smiling spring-time.
        Shoheen sho lo,
        Shoheen hoo lo!

I'd hush my boy beside the fountain,
By the soothing, silvery fountain,
On the pleasant, purple mountain,
    In the sultry summer.
        Shoheen sho lo,
        Shoheen hoo lo!

I would smooth my darling's pillow,
By the blue Atlantic billow,
On the shores of Parknasilla,
    In the golden autumn.
        Shoheen sho lo,
        Shoheen hoo lo!

I would soothe my child to slumber,
By the rosy, rustling ember,
Through the days of dark December.
  In the stormy winter.
    Shoheen sho lo,
    Shoheen hoo lo!

May no cruel fairy charm thee!
May no dread banshee alarm thee!
Flood, nor fire, nor sickness harm thee:
  Winter, spring, and summer,—
  Summer, autumn, winter,
    Shoheen sho lo,
    Shoheen hoo lo!

THE FOGGY DEW.

OH! a wan cloud was drawn
O'er the dim, weeping dawn,
As to Shannon's side I returned at last;
And the heart in my breast
For the girl I loved best
Was beating—ah beating, how loud and fast!
While the doubts and the fears
Of the long, aching years
Seemed mingling their voices with the moaning flood:
Till full in my path,
Like a wild water-wraith,
My true love's shadow lamenting stood.

But the sudden sun kissed
The cold, cruel mist
Into dancing showers of diamond dew;
The dark flowing stream
Laughed back to his beam,
And the lark soared singing aloft in the blue;

>   While no phantom of night,
>   But a form of delight
> Ran with arms outspread to her darling boy :
>   And the girl I love best
>   On my wild, throbbing breast
> Hid her thousand treasures, with a cry of joy.

THE CONFESSION.

A LOVELY lass with modest mien
   Stole out one morning early;
The dew-drops glancing o'er the green
   Made all her pathway pearly.
Young Lawrence struck with Cupid's dart,—
   Cupid's dart distressing,—
As through the fields he saw her start,
   Sighed, "She's gone confessing!
O vo! 'twould ease *my* heart
   To earn the father's blessing."

The Father, with a twinkling eye,
   He watched my boyo cunning,
Unnoticed by his colleen's eye
   Behind the bushes running.
"How well," he laughed, "young Lawrence there,
   After all my pressing,
With his sweetheart, I declare,
   Comes at last confessing.

Oho! I'll just take care
   To give the lad a lesson."

The pleasant priest unbarred the door,
   As solemn as a shadow,
"How slow," cried he, "you've come before.
   How hot-foot now, my laddo.
The serious steal with looks sedate,
   Seeking to be shriven,
But you, you're in no fitting state
   Now to be forgiven,
So go within and wait
   With all your thoughts on heaven."

The fair one following in a while
   Made out her faults with meekness;
The priest then asked her with a smile
   Had she no other weakness,
And led with that young Lawrence in;
   Her cheeks were now confessing.
"Well, since 'tis after all a sin
   Easy of redressing,
Here, dear, I'd best begin
   To give you both my blessing."

THE GIRL I LEFT BEHIND ME.

The route has come, we march away,
    Our colours dance before us,
But sorrow's cloud made dark the day
    That from our sweethearts tore us;
My own dear lass she sobbed "adieu,"
    Her loving arms entwined me,
And oft she prayed me to be true
    To the girl I left behind me.

Yes! I'll be true; when steel to steel
    The ranks of war are rolling,
And round us every cannon peal
    A funeral knell is tolling;
Then if from out the battle flame
    A fatal ball should find me,
My dying lips shall bless the name
    Of the girl I left behind me.

But, if in triumph I return
   To tell a soldier's story,
Though proudly on my breast should burn
   The golden cross of glory,
No other maid with magic art
   Shall break the links that bind me
For ever to the faithful heart
   Of the girl I left behind me.

EVA TUOHILL.

Who's not heard of Eva Tuohill,
Munster's purest, proudest jewel—
Queen of Limerick's lovely maidens,
    Cork's colleens, and Galway girls—
With her slender shape that's swimmin'
Like a swan among the women,
With her voice of silver cadence,
    And her crown of clustering curls?

O! the eyes of Eva Tuohill!
Now, why wouldn't Cromwell cruel,
Just have called two centuries later
    With his cannon at Tervoe?
For, one flash of angry azure
Through that silky black embrasure,
And away old Noll should scatter
    With his army out of view.

Is't describe you Eva Tuohill
With the dozenth rapier duel,

Fought to fix her sweet complexion
    And the colour of her hair?
  Is it picture you her figure,
    That's compelled so many a trigger
Take the deadliest direction
    Through the early morning air?

  Well, no wonder, Eva Tuohill!
    Since you're just one glorious jewel
Lit with lovely flying flushes
    From delightful lip to brow;
  Now in dreams your eyes they darkle,
    Now with joy they dance and sparkle:
Now your cheek is bathed in blushes,
    Drowned in dimpled laughter now.

  But your beauty, Eva Tuohill,
    Is no opal false and cruel;
Nor the meteor star deceiving,
    Flashing ruin from above.
  No! but some divinest splendour,
    Out of angels' tear-drops tender
Crystalled, in one Iris weaving
    Faith and Hope and Virgin Love.

'TIS I CAN WEAVE WOOLLEN AND LINEN.

'Tis I can weave woollen and linen,
    The finest folk wear on their backs;
So, girls, come give over your spinnin',
    And wind off your wool and your flax!

Five year at my woollen and linen
    I've woven from mornin' to night,
With a heart that beat heavy beginnin',
    But is leapin' for ever more light.

For with guineas full up is the stockin',
    Sewed safe in the tick of my bed,
And 'tis soon that I'll rest without rockin',
    Since at Shrove with my Willy I'll wed.

MAUREEN, MAUREEN!

Oh! Maureen, Maureen, have you forgotten
  The fond confession that you made to me,
While round us fluttered the white bog cotton,
  And o'er us waved the wild arbutus tree?
Like bits of sky bo-peeping through the bower,
  No sooner were your blue eyes sought than flown,
Till white and fluttering as the cotton flower
  Your slender hand it slipped into my own.

Oh! Maureen, Maureen, do you remember
  The faithful promise that you pledged to me
The night we parted in black December
  Beneath the tempest-tossed arbutus tree,
When faster than the drops from heaven flowing
  Your heavy tears they showered with ceaseless start,
And wilder than the storm-wind round us blowing
  Your bitter sobs they smote upon my heart?

Oh! Maureen, Maureen, for your love only
    I left my father and mother dear;
Within the churchyard they're lying lonely,
    'Tis from their tombstone I've travelled here.
Their only son, you sent me o'er the billow,
    Ochone! though kneeling they implored me stay;
They sickened with no child to smooth their pillow;
    They died. Are you as dead to me as they?

Oh! Maureen, must then the love I bore you—
    Seven lonesome summers of longing trust—
Turn like the fortune I've gathered for you,
    Like treacherous fairy treasure, into dust?
But Maureen bawn asthore, your proud lips quiver;
    Into your scornful eyes the tears they start;
Your rebel hand returns to mine for ever;
    Oh! Maureen, Maureen, never more we'll part.

WHEN I ROSE IN THE MORNING.

When I rose in the morning,
  My heart full of woe,
I implored all the song birds
  Why their mates on the bough
To their pleading gave heeding,
  While Kate still said "No;"
But they made no kind answer
  To a heart full of woe.

Till the wood-quest at noon,
  From the forest below,
He taught me his secret
  So tender and low
Of stealing fond feeling
  With sweet notes of woe,
Coo-cooing so soft
  Through the green leafy row.

The long shadows fell,
    And the sun he sank low,
And again I was pleading
    In the mild evening glow:
"Ah! Kitty, have pity!"
    Then how could she say "No."
So for ever I'm free
    From a heart full of woe.

THE MILL SONG.

Corn is a-sowing
  Over the hill,
The stream is a-flowing,
  Round goes the mill.
    Winding and grinding,
      Round goes the mill;
    Winding and grinding
      Should never stand still.
    The hands that are strongest
      Are welcome here,
    And those that work longest
      Earn the best cheer.

The green corn is hinting
  Over the hill,
Lasses tormenting
  The lads to their fill.
    Winding and grinding, &c.

The gold corn is glinting
  Over the hill:
Lasses consenting,
  Lads have their will.
    Winding and grinding, &c.

Corn is a-carrying
  Into the mill,
Young folk are marrying
  Over the hill.
    Winding and grinding, &c.

From the hands of the shaker
  Again goes the corn,
The old to God's acre
  Gently are borne.
    Winding and grinding, &c.

The green corn is glistening
  Once more with the spring;
Children are christening,
  Glad mothers sing.
    Winding and grinding, &c.

Thus our life runs around,
  Like the mill with its corn,

Young folk are marrying,
Old folk are burying,
   Young folk are born.
      Winding and grinding,
        Round goes the mill :
      Winding and grinding
        Should never stand still.
      The hands that are strongest
        Are welcome here,
      And they that work longest
        Earn the best cheer.

'TIS A PITY I CAN'T SEE MY LOVE.

On his flute of gold the blackbird bold
Love's tale to his melting mate has told,
   And now the thieves have started;
And o'er the ground, in fluttering round,
Enamoured fly, whilst you and I
   In lonesome pain are parted.
But when hearts beat true through the night of sorrow,
They're blest the more when the magic morrow
   Its rosy ray has darted.
Fortune may wave her wings and fly,
But she'll flutter back again by and by,
   And crown the constant-hearted.

These birds that pair in the April air
Forget their faith on the branches bare,
   By autumn blasts affrighted,
And to fresh loves sing with the start of spring;
When you and I with a golden ring
   In joy shall be united.

For when hearts beat true through the night of sorrow,
They're blest the most when the marriage morrow
    Its lamp of love has lighted.
    Fortune may wave her wings and fly,
    But she'll flutter back to us by and by,
    And crown the troth we've plighted.

WITH THE NORTH.

With lip contemptuous curling,
 She cried, "Is freedom's flag above
Fold on fold unfurling,
 And Patrick pleading love?
Oh! yes, when patriots hand in hand
Unite to free their foster-land
From slavery's accursed band,
 What true man woos a woman?
Then with my bitter scorning
 Go, live dishonoured, die a slave,
Or march to-morrow morning
 To battle with the brave."

"We'll steal a march on sorrow,"
 Our Captain sighed, a soldier grey,
"Sound the drum to-morrow
 Before the dawn of day."

But ere the drum's first muffled beat
The women crowded down the street,
How many never more to meet
   Their death-devoted heroes.
Then as I passed her dwelling,
   My proud one o'er her casement frame.
The sobs her bosom swelling,
   Leant forth and sighed my name.

Oh! have you seen Atlantic
   Advance his green, resistless line
Against the cliffs gigantic,
   And bury them in brine?
Thus on our stubborn foe we fell,
Death's lightning darting from our steel,
Whilst round us every cannon peal
   A hero's requiem thundered!
And still with forward faces
   Went down in death our dauntless men.
And still into their places
   As gallant hearts stepped in.

Till to a sunburst glorious,
   That all the field of battle fired,

Before our van victorious
    The sullen South retired.
Then peace returned, and from the war
Our banner bright with many a star
'Twas mine to flutter from afar
    In triumph to our city;
Till I at last could wreathe it
    Around my true love's throbbing heart,
And we two kissed beneath it,
    Oh! never more to part.

NANCY, THE PRIDE OF THE WEST.

WE have dark lovely looks on the shores where the Spanish
    From their gay ships came gallantly forth,
And the sweet shrinking violets sooner will vanish
    Than modest blue eyes from our north;
But oh! if the fairest of fair-daughtered Erin
    Gathered round at her golden request,
There's not one of them all that she'd think worth comparing
    With Nancy, the pride of the west.

You'd suspect her the statue the Greek fell in love with,
    If you chanced on her musing alone,
Or some goddess great Jove was offended above with,
    And chilled to a sculpture of stone;
But you'd think her no colourless, classical statue,
    When she turned from her pensive repose,
With her glowing grey eyes glancing timidly at you,
    And the blush of a beautiful rose.

Have you heard Nancy sigh? then you've caught the sad echo
    From the wind harp enchantingly borne.

Have you heard the girl laugh? then you've heard the first
    cuckoo
  Carol summer's delightful return.
And the songs that poor ignorant country folk fancy
    The lark's liquid raptures on high,
Are just old Irish airs from the sweet lips of Nancy,
    Flowing up and refreshing the sky.

And though her foot dances so soft from the heather
    To the dew-twinkling tussocks of grass,
It but warns the bright drops to slip closer together
    To image the exquisite lass;
We've no men left among us, so lost to emotion,
    Or scornful, or cold to her sex,
Who'd resist her, if Nancy once took up the notion
    To set that soft foot on their necks.

Yet, for all that the bee flies for honey-dew fragrant
    To the half-opened flower of her lips,
And the butterfly pauses, the purple-eyed vagrant,
    To play with her pink finger-tips;
From all human lovers she locks up the treasure
    A thousand are starving to taste,
And the fairies alone know the magical measure
    Of the ravishing round of her waist.

JENNY, I'M NOT JESTING.

"Ah, Jenny, I'm not jesting,
 Believe what I'm protesting,
 And yield what I'm requesting
  These seven years through."
"Ah, Lawrence, I may grieve you;
 Yet, if I can't relieve you,
 Sure, why should I deceive you
  With words untrue.
 But, since you must be courtin',
 There's Rosy and her fortune,
 'Tis rumoured your consortin'
  With her of late.
 Or there's your cousin Kitty,
 So charming and so witty,
 She'd wed you out of pity,
  Kind Kate."

"Fie! Jenny, since I knew you,
　Of all the lads that woo you,
　None's been so faithful to you,
　　If truth were told;
　Even when yourself was dartin'
　Fond looks at fickle Martin,
　Till off the thief went startin'
　　For Sheela's gold."

"And, if you've known me longest,
　Why should your love be strongest,
　And his that's now the youngest,
　　For that be worst?"
"Fire, Jenny, quickest kindled
　Is always soonest dwindled,
　And thread the swiftest spindled
　　Snaps first."

"If that's your wisdom, Larry,
　The longer I can tarry,
　The luckier I shall marry
　　At long, long last."
"I've known of girls amusing,
　Their minds, the men refusing,
　Till none were left for choosing
　　At long, long last."

"Well, since it seems that marriage
 Is still the safest carriage,
 And all the world disparage
  The spinster lone ;
 Since you might still forsake me,
 I think I'll let you take me.
 Yes ! Larry, you may make me
  Your own ! "

THE HOUR WE PARTED.

The hour we parted,
When broken-hearted
You clung around me,
    Maureen, aroo,
I swore I'd treasure,
Thro' pain and pleasure,
Thro' health and sickness,
    My love for you.

And still that jewel,
Thro' changes cruel
Of fickle Fortune
    I'll jealous guard;
Still let her vary,
The jade contràry,
If but my Mary
    Be my reward.

Yes! scorn and anger,
Distress and languor,
They're welcome willing,
   The long day thro',
Could I feel certain
That ev'ning's curtain
But clos'd us nearer,
   Maureen, aroo!

The dreamy shadows
Along the meadows
Go softly stealing,
   And falls the dew;
And o'er the billows,
Like faithful swallows,
All, all my thoughts, dear,
   Fly home to you.

With touches silken,
I see you milkin'
The crossest Kerry
   In Adragole;
And like a fairy,
You're singing, Mary,

Till every keeler
   Is foaming full.

The night is falling,
And you are calling
The cattle homeward,
   With coaxing tone;
In God's own keeping,
Awake or sleeping,
'Tis now I leave you,
   Maureen, mavrone!

THE SMITH'S SONG.

Ding dong, didilium ! the big sledge is swinging,
Ding dong, didilium ! the little hammer's ringing.
Ding dong, didilium ! set the bellows snoring :
Ding dong, didilium ! the red fire is roaring."

Hush, boys, and hark, boys, I hear a pair eloping,
Hush, boys, and hark, boys, they'll go free, I'm hoping,
Ding dong, didilium ! I hear a shoe clinking,
Ding dong, didilium ! there's need of nails, I'm thinking."

For Heaven's sake, a shoe, smith!" "Your honor, here 'tis
    ready ;
Woa, mare, and so, mare, and steady, girl, steady !
Ding dong, didilium ! off goes the carriage,
Ding dong, didilium ! good luck be with the marriage."

Hush, boys, and hark, boys, I hear the kettle-drumming,
Drimin dhu, drimin dhu,' King James's horse are coming :
Up, on the thatch, where my pretty pikes are hidden,
And have them all handy and bright when you're bidden."

"For Heaven's sake, the pikes, smith!" "They're here
    for your picking,
  Long pikes and strong pikes, and pikes for Dutchmen-
    sticking!
  Ding dong, didilium! cursing in their cruppers,
  Here jog the Mynherrs, 'tis time for our suppers."

MO MOIREEN DHU.

When I sailed away
  To win wealth for you
O'er the stormy sea,
  O mo moireen dhu!
On the western wave
A black pirate knave
Bore me off his slave
  From mo moireen dhu!
And I should work
For the tyrant Turk,
In cruel chains, beneath the scorching sun,
And never hear, when the dreadful week was done,
  Bells for Christian prayer
  Calling through the air.

Till a Moslem maid,
  For the love of me,
With her artful aid,
  Stole and set me free.

But no soft collogue
With that charming rogue,
Mo moireen oge,
   Turned my heart from thee,
And I'm home at last
O'er the ocean vast,
My good red gold, in gaily glittering store,
Into mo moireen's modest lap to pour;
   While with magic swell
   Wakes our marriage bell.

PLERACA.

Beimeedh a gole!
Fill up the bowl,
Let us console
Dull care with a glass, boys!
Shall it be wine,
Fragrant and fine,
Fresh smuggled from Spain underneath a mattràss, boys?
No! all of those pleasant
Casks out of Cadiz
Leave as a present,
Lads, for the ladies!
But for ourselves, sure
What should we say
But Whiskey for ever!
Till dawning of day.

Beimeedh a gole!
Wasn't it droll,

He that first stole
Fire from Heaven's grate, boys,
Look now, was left,
Chained to a cleft,
A century through, for an eagle to ate, boys!
St. Pat, though, when stealing
Fire from that quarter,
Kept it concealing
Snug under water;
Till he'd conveyed it
Safe to the ground,
Then looked, and, begorra,
'Twas *whiskey* he found.

Beimeedh a gole!
Each with his poll
Quite in control,
For all its containing;
Smiling we sit,
Warming our wit
With nectar the Gods might begrudge us the draining.
Now, ere we go snoozing
Under the clothes,
Don't be refusing
One health I propose.

Here's to the darling,
　Pale as the dew,
That pounds Purple Bacchus
　And all of his crew!

SONG OF THE GHOST.

When all were dreaming
  But Pastheen Power,
A light came streaming
  Beneath her bower:
A heavy foot
  At her door delayed,
A heavy hand
  On the latch was laid.

"Now who dare venture,
  At this dark hour,
Unbid to enter
  My maiden bower?"
"Dear Pastheen, open
  The door to me,
And your true lover
  You'll surely see."

"My own true lover,
    So tall and brave,
Lives exiled over
    The angry wave."
"Your true love's body
    Lies on the bier,
His faithful spirit
    Is with you here."

"His look was cheerful,
    His voice was gay;
Your speech is fearful,
    Your face is grey;
And sad and sunken
    Your eye of blue,
But Patrick, Patrick,
    Alas! 'tis you!"

Ere dawn was breaking
    She heard below
The two cocks shaking
    Their wings to crow.
"Oh, hush you, hush you,
    Both red and grey,

Or you will hurry
My love away.

"Oh, hush your crowing,
  Both grey and red,
Or he'll be going
  To join the dead;
Oh, cease from calling
  His ghost to the mould,
And I'll come crowning
  Your combs with gold."

When all were dreaming
  But Pastheen Power,
A light went streaming
  From out her bower;
And on the morrow,
  When they awoke,
They knew that sorrow
  Her heart had broke.

COLLEEN OGE ASTHORE.

When I marched away to war,
How you kissed me o'er and o'er:
    Weeping, pressed me;
    Sobbing, blessed me;
Colleen, colleen oge asthore.

I was wounded, wounded sore,
Dead, your father falsely swore;
    Mad to harry
    You to marry
One with miser-gold in store.

Ah! but when you dreamed me dead,
Forth you flew a wildered maid:
    Ever grieving,
    Ever weaving
Willow, willow for your head.

"Nay, he lives," your mother said,
But you only shook your head;
    "Why deceive me?
    Ah! believe me,
Mother, mother, he is dead."

So you pined and pined away,
Till, when in the winter grey
    Home I hasted,
    Wan and wasted,
Colleen, colleen oge, you lay.

"'Tis his lonesome ghost," you said,
"Come to call me to the dead;"
    "Nay, discover
    Your dear lover
Longing now at last to wed."

Then your cheek, so pale before,
With the rose of hope once more,
    Faintly, slowly,
    Brightly, wholly,
Blossomed, colleen oge asthore.

Till upon the chapel floor,
Side by side, we knelt and swore,
    Duty dearest,
    Love sincerest,
Colleen, colleen oge asthore.

THE FLIGHT OF THE EARLS

To other shores across the sea
    We speed with swelling sail;
Yet still there lingers on our lee
    A phantom Innisfail.
Oh fear, fear not, gentle ghost,
    Your sons shall turn untrue!
Though fain to fly your lovely coast,
    They leave their hearts with you.

As slowly into distance dim
    Your shadow sinks and dies,
So o'er the ocean's utmost rim
    Another realm shall rise;
New hills shall swell, new vales expand,
    New rivers winding flow,
But could we for a foster land
    Your mother-love forego?

Shall mighty Espan's martial praise
    Our patriot pulses still,
And o'er your memory's fervent rays
    Forever cast a chill?
Oh, no! we live for your relief,
    Till home from alien earth
We share the smile that gilds your grief,
    The tear that gems your mirth.

KITTY BHAN.

BEFORE the first ray of blushing day,
   Who should come by but Kitty bhan,
With her cheek like the rose on a bed of snows,
   And her bosom beneath like the sailing swan.
   I looked and looked till my heart was gone.

With the foot of the fawn she crossed the lawn,
   Half confiding and half in fear;
And her eyes of blue they thrilled me through,
   One blessèd minute; then like the deer,
   Away she darted, and left me here.

Oh! Sun, you are late at your golden gate,
   For you've nothing to show beneath the sky
To compare to the lass who crossed the grass
   Of the shamrock field ere the dew was dry,
   And the glance that she gave me as she went by.

THE WHITE BLOSSOM 'S OFF THE BOG.

The white blossom 's off the bog, and the leaves are off the trees,
And the singing birds have scattered across the stormy seas :
        And oh ! 'tis winter,
        Wild, wild winter !
With the lonesome wind sighing for ever through the trees.

How green the leaves were springing ! how glad the birds were singing !
When I rested in the meadow with my head on Patrick's knees:
        And oh ! 'twas spring time,
        Sweet, sweet spring time !
With the daisies all dancing before in the breeze.

With the spring the fresh leaves they'll laugh upon the trees,
And the birds they'll flutter back with their songs across the seas.
But I'll never rest again with my head on Patrick's knees ;
        And for me 'twill be winter,
        All the year winter,
With the lonesome wind sighing for ever through the trees.

WITH FLUTTERING JOY.

How happy for the little birds
    From tree to tree, away and hither,
To pour their pretty, warbling words,
    And fly with fluttering joy together!
But let the sun rejoice the skies,
    Or sullen clouds his glory smother,
With heavy hearts we still must rise
    Far, far away from one another.

Now leave those foolish, feathered things,
    O Fortune, Fortune, fond and cruel!
And fit two pair of trusty wings
    Upon myself and Mary jewel,
That she and I from earth may start,
    And skim the sky on angel feather,
Till from mid-heaven, heart to heart
    With fluttering joy we fall together.

A SAILOR LOVED A FARMER'S DAUGHTER.

A SAILOR once wooed a farmer's daughter,
    The fairest lass in all the country side.
She loved him well; but when he besought her
    With beating, beating heart to be his bride,
"A sailor lad," she said, "I'll never, never wed,
    And live a wife and widow all in one;
O no, my charmer shall be a farmer,
    Returning faithful with the set of sun."

At danger's call, across the water
    The sailor went, but left his heart behind:
Fresh lovers whispered the farmer's daughter;
    Yet when they prayed her to confess her mind,
"A farmer's lad," she said, "I'll never, never wed,
    When heroes bleed to guard their native strand.
Till war is over I need no lover:
    Then let the stoutest soldier claim my hand."

When peace returned, escaped from slaughter,
    With stars and crosses home our warriors came,
And some went wooing the farmer's daughter,
    But none could charm the lass to change her name;
Until once more from far a gallant, gallant tar
    Began with beating heart his love to tell;
And sweetly turning, with blushes burning,
    She sighed: "Since first we met I've loved you well!

THE REAPER'S REVENGE.

Often I dream of the day, asthore,
  With secret sighs and laughter,
When you went reaping the oats before,
  And I came gathering after.
And tenderly, tenderly with the corn
  Looks of love you threw me;
Till I stood up with eyes of scorn
  And withered your hopes to woo me.

Often and often I'm dreaming still,
  With tears and smiles together,
Of the month I stretched so weak and ill
  In the wild and wintry weather.
While tenderly, tenderly, you would tap
  To know the news of Nora;
Till I grew fonder of your rap
  Than my father's voice, acora!

But most I remember the plan concealed
    That through the spring amused you,
To watch till you found me in the field
    Where in autumn I refused you,
Then earnestly, earnestly, in my eyes
    To gaze, till I returned you
The look of looks and the sigh of sighs,
    On the spot where once I spurned you.

THE BLUE, BLUE SMOKE.

Oh, many and many a time
　In the dim old days,
When the chapel's distant chime
　Pealed the hour of evening praise,
I've bowed my head in prayer;
　Then shouldered scythe or bill,
And travelled free of care
　To my home across the hill;
　　Whilst the blue, blue smoke
　　Of my cottage in the coom,
　　　Softly wreathing,
　　　Sweetly breathing,
　　Waved my thousand welcomes home.

For oft and oft I've stood,
　Delighted in the dew,
Looking down across the wood,
　Where it stole into my view—
Sweet spirit of the sod,
　Of our own Irish earth,

Going gently up to God
 From the poor man's hearth.
  O, the blue, blue smoke
  Of my cottage in the coom,
   Softly wreathing,
   Sweetly breathing,
  My thousand welcomes home.

But I hurried swiftly on,
 When Herself from the door
Came swimming like a swan
 Beside the Shannon shore;
And after her in haste,
 On pretty, pattering feet,
Our rosy cherubs raced
 Their daddy dear to meet;
  While the blue, blue smoke
  Of my cottage in the coom,
   Softly wreathing,
   Sweetly breathing,
  Waved my thousand welcomes home.

But the times are sorely changed
 Since those dim old days,

And far, far I've ranged
   From those dear old ways;
And my colleen's golden hair
   To silver all has grown,
And our little cherub pair
   Have cherubs of their own;
      And the black, black smoke,
      Like a heavy funeral plume,
         Darkly wreathing,
         Fearful breathing,
      Crowns the city with its gloom.

But 'tis our comfort sweet,
   Through the long toil of life,
That we'll turn with tired feet
   From the noise and the strife,
And wander slowly back
   In the soft western glow,
Hand in hand by the track
   That we trod long ago;
      Till the blue, blue smoke
      Of our cottage in the coom,
         Softly wreathing,
         Sweetly breathing,
      Waves our thousand welcomes home.

RUSTIC POEMS.

FATHER O'FLYNN.

Of priests we can offer a charmin' variety,
Far renowned for larnin' and piety;
Still, I'd advance ye widout impropriety,
   Father O'Flynn as the flower of them all.

Chorus.

Here's a health to you, Father O'Flynn,
Slainté, and slainté, and slainté agin ;
   Powerfulest preacher, and
   Tinderest teacher, and
Kindliest creature in ould Donegal.

Don't talk of your Provost and Fellows of Trinity,
Famous for ever at Greek and Latinity,
Faix and the divels and all at Divinity,

Father O'Flynn 'd make hares of them all!
Come, I vinture to give ye my word,
Never the likes of his logic was heard,
    Down from mythology
    Into thayology,
'Troth! and conchology if he'd the call.

Chorus.

Here's a health to you, Father O'Flynn,
Slainté, and slainté, and slainté agin:
    Powerfulest preacher, and
    Tinderest teacher, and
Kindliest creature in ould Donegal.

Och! Father O'Flynn you've the wonderful way wid
All ould sinners are wishful to pray wid you,
All the young childer are wild for to play wid you,
    You've such a way wid you, Father avick!
    Still for all you've so gentle a soul,
    Gad, you've your flock in the grandest control:
        Checking the crazy ones,
        Coaxin' onaisy ones,
Liftin' the lazy ones on wid the stick.

Chorus.

Here's a health to you, Father O'Flynn,
Slainté, and slainté, and slainté agin :
    Powerfulest preacher, and
    Tinderest teacher, and
Kindliest creature in ould Donegal.

And though quite avoidin' all foolish frivolity,
Still at all seasons of innocent jollity,
Where was the play-boy could claim an equality
  At comicality, Father, wid you?
    Once the Bishop looked grave at your jest,
    Till this remark set him off wid the rest :
      " Is it lave gaiety
      All to the laity?
  Cannot the clargy be Irishmen too?"

Chorus.

Here's a health to you, Father O'Flynn,
Slainté, and slainté, and slainté agin ;
    Powerfulest preacher, and
    Tinderest teacher, and
Kindliest creature in ould Donegal.

MOLLEEN OGE.

Molleen oge, my Molleen oge,
 Go put on your natest brogue,
And slip into your smartest gown,
 You rosy little rogue;
 For a message kind I bear
 To yourself from ould Adair,
That Pat the piper 's come around,
 And there'll be dancin' there.
  Oh, my Molleen,
  Oh, my colleen,
  We'll dance to Pat,
  And after that
 Collogue upon one chair.

Molleen dear, I'd not presume,
 To encroach into your room,
But I'd forgot a fairin'
 I'd brought you from Macroom;

So open, and I swear
Not one peep upon you; there!
'Tis a silver net to gather
At the glass your goolden hair.
  Oh, my Molleen,
  Oh, my colleen,
  We'll dance to Pat,
  And after that
Collogue upon one chair.

Molleen pet, my Molleen pet,
Faix, I'm fairly in a fret
At the time you're tittivatin';
Molleen, aren't you ready yet?
Now net and gown and brogue
Are you sure you're quite the vogue?
But, bedad, you look so lovely,
I'll forgive you, Molleen oge.
  Oh, my Molleen,
  Oh, my colleen,
  We'll dance to Pat,
  And after that
Upon one chair collogue.

———

TWO IRISH IDYLLS.

I.—RIDING DOUBLE.

Trottin' to the fair,
   Me and Moll Malony,
Sated, I declare,
   On a single pony;
How am I to know that
   Molly's safe behind,
Wid our heads, in oh! that
   Awk'ard way inclined?
By her gintle breathin',
   Whispered past my ear,
And her white arms wreathin'
   Warm around me *here*.
Trottin' to the fair,
   Me and Moll Malony,
Sated, I declare,
   On a single pony.

Yerrig! Masther Jack,
   Lift your fore-legs higher,

Or a rousin' crack
    Surely you'll require.
"Ah!" says Moll, "I'm frightened
    That the pony 'll start,"
And her hands she tightened
    On my happy heart;
Till, widout reflectin',
    'Twasn't quite the vogue,
Somehow, I'm suspectin'
    That I snatched a pogue.
Trottin' to the fair,
    Me and Moll Malony,
Sated, I declare,
    On a single pony.

II.—RIDING TREBLE.

Joultin' to the fair,
    Three upon the pony,
That so lately were
    Me and Moll Malony.
"How can three be on, boy?
    Sure, the wife and you,
Though you should be *wan*, boy,
    Can't be more nor *two*."

Arrah, now, then may be
   You've got eyes to see
That this purty baby
   Adds us up to *three*.
Joultin' to the fair
   Three upon the pony,
That so lately were
   Me and Moll Malony.

Come, give over, Jack,
   Cap'rin' and curvettin',
All that's on your back
   Foolishly forgettin';
For I've tuk the notion
   Wan may cant'rin' go,
Trottin' is a motion
   I'd extind to *two;*
But to travel steady
   Matches best wid *three*,
And we're that already,
   Mistress Moll and me.
Joultin' to the fair
   Three upon the pony,
That so lately were
   Me and Moll Malony.

FAN FITZGERL.

  Wirra, wirra! ologone!
  Can't ye lave a lad alone,
Till he's proved there's no tradition left of any other girl,—
  Not even Trojan Helen,
  In beauty all excellin',—
Who's been up to half the divlement of Fan Fitzgerl.

  Wid her brows of silky black
  Arched above for the attack,
Her eyes they dart such azure death on poor admirin' man:
  Masther Cupid, point your arrows,
  From this out, agin the sparrows,
For your bested at Love's archery by young Miss Fan.

  See what showers of goolden thread
  Lift and fall upon her head,
The likes of such a trammel-net at say was niver spread:
  For whin accurately reckoned,
  'Twas computed that each second
Of her curls has cot a Kerryman and kilt him dead.

Now mintion, if ye will,
Brandon Mount and Hungry Hill,
Or Ma'g'llicuddy's Reeks renowned for cripplin' all they
Still the country side confisses
None of all its precipices
Cause a quarther of the carnage of the nose of Fan.

But your shatthered hearts suppose
Safely steered apast her nose,
She's a current and a reef beyant to wreck them rovin' s
My maning it is simple,
For that current is her dimple,
And the cruel reef 'twill coax ye to 's her coral lips.

I might inform ye further
Of her bosom's snowy murther,
And an ankle ambuscadin' through her gown's delightful
But what need, when all the village
Has forsook its peaceful tillage,
And flown to war and pillage all for Fan Fitzgerl!

BAT OF THE BRIDGE.

On the bridge of Dereen,
   Away up by Killarney,
You'll be sure to be seein'
   Poor Batsy O'Kearney
A big stick in the air
   So lazily swingin',
Smokin' and jokin'
   And carelessly singin'
Some snatch of a song,
   Out over the river,
As it rushes along
   For iver and iver
To the Bay of Kenmare.

    Six feet six
    Is the fix
    Of his height,
    Honour bright!

Forty-eight the diminsion
Round his ribs by my inchin';
It's murther to say
Such a man's thrun away.

He's the last to delay
   And the earliest comer
On the bridge by the bay,
   Winter and summer.
Do you question why so?
   What keeps him for iver
Smokin' and jokin'
   And out on the river
That rushes below,
   Serenadin' so gaily?
'Twas the cowardly blow
   Of a tinker's shillelagh
Left the proper man so.

But you're wonderin', why,
   How at all it could happen
Such a broth of a boy
   Got the scandalous rappin'.
'Twas September fair day,
   And the Adragole faction

Wid Dereen for the green
   And the bridge were in action;
And from off the bridge road,
   Wid his cudgel so clever,
Bat was leatherin' a load
   Of Cork men for ever,
Just as if it was play.

When up from beneath,
   Still further and further,
Houldin' tight in his teeth
   A stick that was murther,
That black tinker stole,
   By the ivy boughs clingin',
On the edge of the bridge
   The knees softly swingin';
And, unknownst at his back,
   From the wall of the river
Fetched O'Kearney a crack,
   That left him for iver
Wid a poor, puzzled poll.

Did he fall? Not at all!
   But he picked off that tinker

Like a snail from the wall;
    And before you could think, or
Repate your own name,
    Cot the stick from the ruffi'n,
Knocked him dead on the head,
    And widout shroud or coffin
Tossed him into the tide.
    And his black corpse for ever
From Ireland should glide,
    For her good soil could never
Cover up such a shame.

Thin backward agin,
    Wid a bitter screech flyin',
On the Adragole men,
    Just as they were cryin',
"The bridge is our own."
    In their thick, like a flail, he
Swung, till it sung,
    The tinker's shillelagh;
So that staggerin' down,
    Broken and batthered,
Out of the town
    All Adragole scatthered
Before Batsy alone.

Ever since which,
   Poor Bat's only iday
Is to sit on the bridge,
   Wet day or dry day,
Wid that stick in his fist;
   And no tinkerin' fellas
Dare to come there
   Wid their pots and their bellas,
And all Adragole
   Takes the ford down the river,
For fear that the fool
   On the bridge-end for iver
Should give them a twist.

So he's come by a name,
   The English of which, sir,
Translatin' that same,
   Is "Bat of the Bridge," sir.
But the hour's growin' late;
   Good night, and safe journey!
It's afloat in your boat
   You should be, Doctor Corney.
By myself, now, bad scran
   To the tribe of the tinkers,

For they've left a good man,
   Like a horse widout blinkers,
All bothered and bate.

    Six feet six
    Is the height
Of poor Batsy to-night,
Forty-eight the diminsion
Round his ribs by my inchin';
It's murther, I say,
Such a man's thrun away.

THE LIGHT IN THE SNOW.

Oh Pat, the bitter day when you bravely parted from us,
    The mother and myself on the cruel quays of Cork :
When you took the long kiss, and you gave the faithful promise
    That you'd soon bring us over to be wid you at New York.

But the times they grew worse through the wild, weary winter,
    And my needle all we had to find livin' for us two ;
While the mother drooped and drooped till I knelt down fore-
        nint her
    And closed her dyin' eyes, dear,—but still no word of you.

Then the neighbours thought you false to me but I knew you
        better,
    Though the bud became the leaf, and the corn began to start :
And the swallow she flew back, and still sorra letter,
    But I sewed on and on, Pat, and kep' a stout heart.

Till the leaves they decayed, and the rook and the starlin'
    Returned to the stubble, and I'd put by enough
To start at long last in search of my darlin'
    Alone across the ocean so unruly and rough.

Until at the end, very weak and very weary,
    I reached the overside, and started on my search;
But no account for ever of Patrick for his Mary,
    By advertisin' for you, dear, or callin' you in church.

Yet still I struggled on, though my heart was almost broken
    And my feet torn entirely on the rough, rugged stone;
Till that day it came round, signs by and by token,
    The day five year that we parted you, mavrone.

Oh! the snow it was sweepin' through the dark, silent city,
    And the cruel wind it cut through my thin, tattered gown.
Still I prayed the good God on his daughter to take pity;
    When a sudden, strange light shone forenint me up the town.

And the light it led on till at last right oppossite
    A large, lonely house it vanished as I stood;
Wid my heart axing wildly of me, was it, oh, was it
    A warnin' of ill or a token of good.

When the light kindled up agin, brighter and bigger,
  And the shadow of a woman across the windy passed :
While close, close, and closer to her stole a man's figure,
  And I fainted, as you caught me in your true arms at last.

Then Pat, my own Pat, I saw that you were altered
  To the shadow of yourself by the fever on the brain :
While "Mary, Mary darlin'," at last your lips they faltered,
  "You've given your poor Patrick his mem'ry back again."

And the good, gentle priest, when he comes, is never weary
  Of sayin', as he spakes of that light in the snow,
"The Lord heard your prayer, and in pity for you, Mary,
  Restored Pat the raison that he lost long ago."

WHAT IS LIFE WIDOUT A WIFE?

FESTAL CHORUS.

The Boys.

What is life widout a wife?

The Girls.

'Tis the bee widout his honey;
'Tis the hoard by misers stored;
'Tis the spendthrift's waste of money;
Spring and all her song-birds mute;
Summer wid no rosy flowers;
Autumn robbed of all his fruit;
Winter—and no fireside hours.

The Girls.

What is life widout a husband?

The Boys.

Poetry widout an *iday;*
Powdther, and the shot forgot;
Fish—and it foriver Friday;

Musha ! night widout a moon ;
    Faix ! and fever widout physic ;
Troth ! and music out of tune ;
    'Dad ! and dancin' widout music.

The Girls.

Then, give over playin' rover,
    Lads, wid Jacky-Lanthern Folly,
Fondly turnin' to the burnin'
    Of Love's beacon bright and holy.

The Boys.

Now, girls, dear, whisper here !
    Where 'll we find his guidin' beacon.

The Girls.

In the skies of woman's eyes
    Fondly look, and one will waken.

The Boys.

Och ! then you coquettes unthrue,
    To one lad at last be list'nin',
Whilst your rose of beauty blows—
    Whilst like goold your hair is glist'nin',

Yes! your charms into our arms
　　Yield, whilst you can still be patrons,
Or too late you'll mourn your fate,
　　Poor ould maids among the matrons.

THE WRECK OF THE AIDEEN.

Is it cure me, docther, darlin'? an ould boy of siventy-four,
Afther soakin' off Berehaven three and thirty hour and more,
Wid no other navigation underneath me but an oar.

God incrase ye, but it's only half myself is livin' still,
An' there's mountin' slow but surely to my heart the dyin' chill;
God incrase ye for your goodness, but I'm past all mortial skill.

But ye'll surely let them lift me, won't you, docther, from below?
Ye'll let them lift me surely—very soft and very slow—
To see my ould ship, Aideen, wanst agin before I go?

Lay my head upon your shoulder; thank ye kindly, docther, dear.
Take me now; God bless ye, cap'n! now together! sorra fear!
Have no dread that ye'll distress me—now, agin, ochone! I see her.

Ologone! my Aideen's Aideen, christened by her laughin' lips,
Wid a sprinkle from her finger as ye started from the slips,
Thirty year ago come Shrovetide, like a swan among the ships.

And we both were constant to ye till the bitter, bitter day,
Whin the typhus took my darlin', and she pined and pined away,
Till yourself's the only sweetheart that was left me on the say.

So through fair and foul we'd travel, you and I thin, usen't we;
The same ould coorse from Galway Bay, by Limerick and Tralee,
Till this storm it shook me overboard, and murthered you, machree.

But now, agra, the unruly wind has flown into the west,
And the silver moon is shinin' soft upon the ocean's breast,
Like Aideen's smilin' spirit come to call us to our rest.

Still the sight is growin' darker, and I cannot rightly hear;
The say's too cold for one so old; O, save me, cap'n, dear!
Now its growin' bright and warm agin, and Aideen, Aideen's here.

THE HANDSOME WITCH.

"Have I seen a witch, your honour?
    'Deed I often have that same;
But the worst was Morna Connor,
    Called 'The Handsome Witch' by name.
She was tall, no woman taller
    Ever cross'd your cur'ous sight,
And to see her pass, you'd call her
    Higher nor her proper height:
For though Time his constant quarrel
    Waged upon her cheek and lip;
Though he stole their laughin' coral
    And destroyed their lovely clip;
Though he robbed the sculptured roundness
    From her ivory neck and arm,
Wasted up the soft profoundness
    Of her bosom's swellin' charm;

Silvered her black head wid sprinkles
   Of his shinin' winter snow;
Yes! and wrote his warnin' wrinkles
   On her bold, unbendin' brow—
Time himself, that still unsparin'
   Bows the lordliest in the land,
Could not curb the haughty bearin'
   Of that woman great and grand.
No! nor thin one curlin' cluster
   Of her long, luxuriant hair:
No! nor quinch the steady lustre
   Of her eyes' contimptuous stare.
Many a cow wid swellin' udder,
   As the crafty crone went by,
Took one cowld, unchristian shudder,
   Dad! and ran complately dry;
While the witch she crossed the clover,
   Steadyin' on her skull wid care
A full keeler frothin' over,
   As if milked from out the air.
Many a colleen in the dairy
   Still should wave the churn-staff round,
Scatterin' salt that crabbed fairy
   Wid her canthrips to confound:

But in vain she'd thry for butter,
  Till she hadn't strength to stand;
While through clear, enchanted water
  Morna drew the dead-man's hand.
But I beg your honour's pardon,
  I'll conclude some other day;
For the calf is in the garden,
  And the heifer 's at the hay."

SAVING THE TURF.

Cuttin' the turf, cuttin' the turf, with our feet on the shinin' slan !
Cuttin' the turf, cuttin' the turf, till the cows come home to the bawn !
Footin' the turf, footin' the turf, footin' and turnin' our best,
Footin' the turf, turnin' the turf, till the rook flies home to her nest !
Settin' the turf, settin' the turf, hither and over the land,
Settin' the turf, settin' the turf, till the say-turn sinks on the strand !
Drawin' the turf, drawin' the turf, with our ponies and asses away,
Drawin' the turf, drawin' the turf, till the boats are out in the bay !
Rickin' the turf, rickin' the turf, safe in the haggard at last,
To keep and to comfort us all from the rage of the rain and the blast.

LOOBEEN.

Bridgid.

Ere the sun began to peep,
    Out I wandered through our orchard.

Rosy.

Since you couldn't quiet sleep,
    By the thoughts of Torlogh tortured;
For 'tis rumoured how of late,
    By his manly beauty melted,
With your pippen, plump and straight
    At the boy in vain you pelted.

Bridgid.

Yes! Saint Bridgid, for my sake
    Interferin' with that apple,
Rolled it on to Rory Blake,
    And we're goin' to the chapel.

Rosy.

So you've handsome Rory fast!
    Girls, go set the secret spreadin',
That when solemn Lent is past
    We shall dance at Bridgid's weddin'!
Now, since all her news is out,
    Nora, see can you discover,
Eastward, westward, north, or sout',
    Where's the boy I'd make my lover?

Nora.

Murt na mo you wish to wed.

Rosy.

Now that notion just be sparin'!
With a hornet at my head
    I'd as soon hop over Erin.
Come, I'll give a handsome hint,
    Girls, should set you rightly guessin'.
How is this? To school I wint,
    Till my master learnt my lesson.

Nora.

At the night-school—I've the whole—
    With her make-believe-be-learnin',

'Tis the model-teacher's poll
  That complately she's been turnin'.

Rosy.

Yes! I've clever Phelim fast.

Nora.

  Girls, go set the secret spreadin',
That when solemn Lent is past
  We shall dance at Rosy's weddin'!

THE BLACK '46.

A RETROSPECT.

Out away across the river,
    Where the purple mountains meet,
There's as green a wood as iver,
    Fenced you from the flamin' heat.
And oppòsite, up the mountain,
    Seven ancient cells ye'll see,
And, below, a holy fountain
    Sheltered by a sacred tree;
While between, across the tillage,
    Two boreens full up wid broom
Draw ye down into a village
    All in ruin on the coom;
For the most heart-breakin' story
    Of the fearful famine year
On the silent wreck before ye
    You may read charàctered clear.

Yous are young, too young for ever
   To rec'llect the bitter blight,
How it crep across the River
   Unbeknownst beneath the right;
Till we woke up in the mornin',
   And beheld our country's curse
Wave abroad its heavy warnin',
   Like the white plumes of a hearse.

To our gardens, heavy-hearted,
   In that dreadful summer's dawn,
Young and ould away we started
   Wid the basket and the slan.
But the heart within the bosom
   Gave one leap of awful dread
At each darlin' pratee blossom,
   White and purple, lyin' dead.
Down we dug, but only scattered
   Poisoned spuds along the slope;
Though each ridge in vain it flattered
   Our poor hearts' revivin' hope.
But the desperate toil we'd double
   On into the evenin' shades;
Till the earth to share our trouble
   Shook beneath our groanin' spades;

Till a mist across the meadows
    From the graveyard rose and spread,
And 'twas rumoured ghostly shadows,
    Phantoms of our fathers dead,
Moved among us, wildly sharin'
    In the women's sobs and sighs,
And our stony, still despairin',
    Till night covered up the skies.
Thin we knew for bitter certain
    That the vinom-breathin' cloud,
Closin' still its cruel curtain,
    Surely yet would be our shroud.
And the fearful sights did folly,
    Och! no voice could rightly tell,
But that constant, melancholy
    Murmur of the passin' bell;
Till to toll it none among us
    Strong enough at last was found,
And a silence overhung us
    Awfuller nor any sound.

ANGLO-IRISH BALLADS.

SHUILE AGRA.

(*See* Notes.)

His hair was black, his eye was blue :
His arm was stout, his word was true ;
I wish in my heart I was with you,
    Gotheen mavourneen slaun.
    Shuile, shuile, shuile agra,
    Only death can ease my woe,
    Since the lad of my heart from me did go,
    Gotheen mavourneen slaun.

'Tis oft I sat on my true love's knee ;
Many a fond story he told to me ;
He told me things that ne'er shall be,
    Gotheen mavourneen slaun.
    Shuile, shuile, shuile agra,
    Only death can ease my woe,
    Since the lad of my heart from me did go,
    Gotheen mavourneen slaun.

I sold my rock, I sold my reel;
When my flax was spun, I sold my wheel,
To buy my love a sword of steel,
   Gotheen mavourneen slaun.
   Shuile, shuile, shuile agra,
   Only death can ease my woe,
   Since the lad of my heart from me did go,
   Gotheen mavourneen slaun.

But when King James was forced to flee,
The Wild Geese spread their wings to sea,
And bore mabouchal far from me,
   Gotheen mavourneen slaun.
   Shuile, shuile, shuile agra,
   Only death can ease my woe,
   Since the lad of my heart from me did go,
   Gotheen mavourneen slaun.

I saw them sail from Brandon hill,
Then down I sat and cried my fill,
That every tear would turn a mill,
   Gotheen mavourneen slaun.
   Shuile, shuile, shuile agra,

Only death can ease my woe,
Since the lad of my heart from me did go,
   Gotheen mavourneen slaun.

I wish the King would return to reign,
And bring my true love back again;
I wish, and wish, but I wish in vain,
   Gotheen mavourneen slaun.
   Shuile, shuile, shuile agra,
Only death can ease my woe,
Since the lad of my heart from me did go,
   Gotheen mavourneen slaun.

I'll dye my petticoat, I'll dye it red,
And round the world I'll beg my bread,
Till I find my love alive or dead,
   Gotheen mavourneen slaun.
   Shuile, shuile, shuile agra.
Only death can ease my woe,
Since the lad of my heart from me did go,
   Gotheen mavourneen slaun.

GRAGALMACHREE.

(*See* Notes.)

At the foot of Newry Mountain, to a stream in the wood
One day I went fishing, and the take was so good
That the very first moment my angle was out
My hook it was fast in a fine plunging trout.

But as down stream I stepped, with my soul full of sport,
On a sudden I chanced on a charming resort:
Where the beeches were bending in beautiful bowers
O'er a velvet-green carpet embroidered with flowers.

And from under that arbour, so cool and so deep,
A colleen's voice chanted that made my heart leap,
For the song that she sang was, "My Lawrence, come hither,
For upon my secret heart you 've put your comether."

I threw down my angle, and, in through the shade,
Stole soft to the side of that young, blooming maid:
O, she's slender in the waist and her face is fair to see,
And her name in plain Irish is, Gragalmachree.

For her tears and her sobs she scarcely could say,
"Ah, Lawrence! ah, Lawrence! what carried you this way
To overhear the secret long lodged in my breast,
And leave me for ever disgraced and distressed?"

Now, comfort you, comfort you, Gragalmachree,
For that little, sweet song was Heaven's music to me,
And God's blessing for ever attend on the thought
That took me fishing trout, till I found myself caught.

And the moon she may darken and the stars lose their light:
And the green plains of Erin they may blacken with blight,
And her mountains all melt in the middle of the sea,
If I ever prove false to my Gragalmachree.

'TWAS PRETTY TO BE IN BALLINDERRY.

(*See* Notes.)

'Twas pretty to be in Ballinderry,
  'Twas pretty to be in Aghalee,
'Twas prettier to be in little Ram's Island,
  Trysting under the ivy tree!
    Ochone, ochone!
    Ochone, ochone!
For often I roved in little Ram's Island,
Side by side with Phelimy Hyland,
And still he'd court me and I'd be coy,
Though at heart I loved him, my handsome boy!

" I'm going," he sighed, "from Ballinderry
  Out and across the stormy sea;
Then if in your heart you love me, Mary,
  Open your arms at last to me."
    Ochone, ochone!
    Ochone, ochone!

I opened my arms; how well he knew me!
I opened my arms and took him to me;
And there, in the gloom of the groaning mast.
We kissed our first and we kissed our last!

'Twas happy to be in little Ram's Island,
   But now 'tis sad as sad can be;
For the ship that sailed with Phelimy Hyland
   Is sunk for ever beneath the sea.
      Ochone, ochone!
      Ochone, ochone!
And 'tis oh! but I wear the weeping willow.
And wander alone by the lonesome billow,
And cry to him over the cruel sea,
" Phelimy Hyland, come back to me!"

MY BONNY CUCKOO.

(*See* Notes.)

My bonny cuckoo, come whisper true!
Around the world I'd rove with you;
I'd rove with you until the next spring,
And still my cuckoo would sweetly sing,—
"Cuckoo! cuckoo!" until the next spring;
"Cuckoo! cuckoo!" until the next spring.

The ash and the hazel shall mourning say,—
"Oh, merry cuckoo, don't fly away!
The winter wind is rude and keen;
Oh, cuckoo, stay and keep us green!
Cuckoo! cuckoo! oh stay! oh stay!
And make the season for ever May!"

The thrush and the robin shall sadly cry,—
"Our bonny cuckoo, oh, do not fly!
For when you spread your speckled wing
We have no longer heart to sing.
Cuckoo, cuckoo, still lead our tune,
And make the season for ever June!"

The lads and the lasses together stand,
And call their cuckoo from off the strand,—
" How can you leave us, bird of love,
With the green below and the blue above?
Oh no! oh no! you shall not go,
With the blue above and the green below."

THE WILLOW TREE.

(*See* Notes.)

Oh, take me to your arms, love, for we alas must part;
Oh, take me to your arms, love, for the pain is at my heart.
She hears not, she cares not, but coldly keeps from me,
While here I lie, alone to die, beneath the willow tree.

My love has blooming beauty, my cheek is deadly wan;
My love has countless riches, my gallant fortune's gone.
This ribbon fair, that bound her hair, is all that's left to me,
While here I lie, alone to die, beneath the willow tree.

I once had gold and silver I thought would never end:
I once had gold and silver, and I thought I had a friend:
My wealth is sped, my friend has fled and stolen my love from me;
While here I lie, alone to die, beneath the willow tree.

JACK THE JOLLY PLOUGHBOY.
(See Notes.)

As Jack the jolly ploughboy was ploughing through his land,
He turned his share and shouted to bid his horses stand.
Then down beside his team he sat, contented as a king,
And Jack he sang his song so sweet he made the mountains
      With his Ta-ran-nan nanty na,
      Sing ta-ran-nan nanty na,
      While the mountains all ringing re-echoed the singing
      Of Ta-ran-nan nanty na.

'Tis said old England's sailors, when wintry tempests roar,
Will plough the stormy waters, and pray for those on shore:
But through the angry winter the share, the share for me,
To drive a steady furrow, and pray for those at sea.
      With my Ta-ran-nan nanty na, &c.

When heaven above is bluest, and earth most green below,
Away from wife and sweetheart the fisherman must go :
But golden seed I'll scatter beside the girl I love,
And smile to hear the cuckoo, and sigh to hear the dove.
      With my Ta-ran-nan nanty na, &c.

'Tis oft the hardy fishers a scanty harvest earn,
And gallant tars from glory on wooden legs return,
But a bursting crop for ever shall dance before my flail :
For I'll live and die a farmer all in the Golden Vale.

     With my Ta-ran-nan nanty na, &c.

JENNY.
(See NOTES.)

With laughing looks I once arose,
   How dark soe'er the day;
Now sadly every sunburst shows,
   For joy has fled away, Jenny;
   For joy has fled away!

Nor flocks nor herds nor store of gold,
   Nor broad estate have I;
If beauty must be bought and sold,
   Alas! I cannot buy, Jenny;
   Alas! I cannot buy.

Yet I'll be rich, if you'll be kind,
   And once again agree
To bear me still in loving mind
   Till I've a home for thee, Jenny;
   A home till death for thee.

THE FOX HUNT.

(See Notes.)

The first morning of March in the year '33,
There was frolic and fun in our own country:
The King's County hunt over meadows and rocks,
Most nobly set out in the search of a fox.
    Hullahoo! harkaway! hullahoo! harkaway!
    Hullahoo! harkaway, boys! away, harkaway!

When they started bold Reynard he faced Tullamore,
Through Wicklow and Arklow along the seashore;
There he brisked up his brush with a laugh, and says he,
" 'Tis mighty refreshing this breeze from the sea."
    Hullahoo! harkaway! hullahoo! harkaway!
    Hullahoo! harkaway, boys! away, harkaway!

With the hounds at his heels every inch of the way,
He led us by sunset right into Roscrea;
Here he ran up a chimney and out of the top,
The rogue he cried out for the hunters to stop
    From their loud harkaway! hullahoo! harkaway!
    Hullahoo! harkaway, boys! away, harkaway!

" 'Twas a long thirsty stretch since we left the seashore.
But, lads, here you've gallons of claret galore :
Myself will make free just to slip out of view,
And take a small pull at my own mountain dew."
   So no more hullahoo! hullahoo! harkaway!
   Hullahoo! harkaway, boys! away, harkaway!

One hundred and twenty good sportsmen went down.
And sought him from Ballyland into Blyboyne;
We swore that we'd watch him the length of the night,
So Reynard, sly Reynard, lay hid till the light.
   Hullahoo! harkaway! hullahoo! harkaway!
   Hullahoo! harkaway, boys! away, harkaway!

But the hills they re-echoed right early next morn
With the cry of the hounds and the call of the horn,
And in spite of his action, his craft, and his skill,
Our fine fox was taken on top of the hill.
   Hullahoo! harkaway! hullahoo! harkaway!
   Hullahoo! harkaway, boys! away, harkaway!

When Reynard he knew that his death was so nigh,
For pen, ink, and paper he called with a sigh ;
And all his dear wishes on earth to fulfil,
With these few dying words he declared his last will,

While we ceased harkaway! hullahoo! harkaway!
Hullahoo! harkaway, boys! away, harkaway!

"Here's to you, Mr. Casey, my Curraghmore estate,
And to you, young O'Brien, my money and plate,
And to you, Thomas Dennihy, my whip, spurs, and cap,
For no leap was so cross that you'd look for a gap."
 And of what he made mention they found it no blank,
 For he gave them a cheque on the National Bank.

FROM THE CELTIC.

THE FAIRY BRANCH.
A BARDIC TALE.
(*See* Notes.)

It chanced upon a time, a magic time,
That Cormac, son of Art, arch-king of Erin.
Strode, musing, from his dun in Liathdrum,
When, lo! a noble youth upon the green,
And in his hand a glittering, fairy branch
With nine bright apples of red gold thereon.

  This was, indeed, the wonder-working bough,
That whoso shook, men wounded unto death
And women travail-tortured sunk to sleep,
Soothed by the low, delicious lullaby
Those golden apples uttered. Nay, no want,
No woe, no weariness endures on earth
That swiftly stabs or slowly wastes the soul,
But this sweet branch once shaken wholly hides
In soft oblivion.   Therefore, spake the king,
" Declare thy coming!   Is that branch thine own ?"
" Yea, sire," the youth replied. " Would'st part with it ?"
" Aye, truly would I, so I won its worth."

"What is the price thou askest?" "The award
 Of mine own mouth." "'Tis thine, yet name it me."
"Then, king, I claim thy wife, thy son, thy daughter,
 Chaste Eithné, gallant Cairbré, winsome Ailbhé."
"Great was the price upon thy fairy branch,
 Yet, for I pledged to thee thy mouth's award,
 I fain must grant it all."
                        Therewith the youth
Resigned the magic bough to Cormac's care,
And this the monarch bore within his dun
To Eithné, and to Cairbré, and to Ailbhé.

"A beauteous treasure hast thou brought us, father,"
 Cried Ailbhé straight. "Small wonder," sighed the kin
"Seeing it cost so dear." "What gave you for it?"
"Thy brother, mother, and thyself, O Ailbhé."
"That price were piteous, if thy words be true,"
 Said Eithné; "for we trust that all the earth
 Contains no treasure thou would'st change us for."
"Alas! I plight you all my kingly word
 That I have given you for this Fairy Bough:"
 King Cormac answered weeping, and declared
 The coming of the Bearer of the Branch.

Now when they proved the bitter tidings true,

Queen Eithné searched the sorrow-smitten face
Of Cormac, and for pity held her peace;
And Cairbré took her hand in his and spake not;
But Ailbhé snatched a gleaming knife, and shore
Close to her head her bright, abundant hair,
With " Father, often hast thou called these curls
Thy golden-branching joy—thus, thus they fall
Before the branch of gold that masters them."

Then dark distress obscured the eyes of all,
And broke in bitter rain upon their cheeks,
And choked the cheerful family of words
With grievous sighs and great heart-bursting groans,
Till Cormac caught the wonder-working bough
And shook it softly o'er them, and forthwith,
Soothed by the low, delicious lullaby
Those golden apples uttered, they forgot
What ill had happ'd them, and arose and went
With smiles to meet the Bearer of the Branch.
Howbeit with tears King Cormac strode before.
When lo the youth! Then Cormac: "See thy price,
The heavy price I pledged thee for this branch."
"Well hast thou kept thy promise; wherefore take
A blessing for thy truth's sake; aye, a blessing
Shall win thee victory." Thus they went their way—

The youth and his companions glad at heart :
The other wifeless, childless, full of woe.

   Now on the morrow, when that mournful news
Was noised abroad through Erin, loud laments
Arose from all the land, but in Teamhair
The loudest, from the princes round the throne
To lowliest labourer in the royal fields ;
So dear beloved was Eithné for her wealth
Of queenly wit and wisdom—dearer still
For constant deeds of thoughtfullest charity ;
So dear beloved was Cairbré for his might
Of manly youth, not lightly roused to wrath,
Yet swift and sure to succour the oppressed ;
So dear beloved was Ailbhé for her dower
Of artless beauty and her voice of song,
That held the blackbirds hushed in Derrycarn.

   These, therefore, all the land with many tears
Bewailing wept ; and tho' their monarch yearned
To share with them his sorrow, ne'ertheless
In pity for his people, once again
He raised the fairy branch of glittering gold
And shook it in their midst, and so subdued
Their grief with glamour, till they smiled again.

Yet Cormac's grief possessed him more and more.
Seeing he mourned alone; and though in court
He ever kept a seeming cheerful face,
Nor lived less instant in his daily round
Of royal duty: yet the thoughtful days
Of law and chess and judgment lightest lay
Upon his suffering spirit. Heavily went
The weekly wassail; sadly shone the dawns
Of race and chase, tho' bright to all beside.
But darkest gloomed the long, lone day of love;
For then within his palace, without food,
He mused, a mournful man; or wandering
From chamber on to chamber, smote
His bosom at the silent spinning wheel,
The stringless harp, or touched with trembling hand
The empty torque of gold, the empty fails
That last had clasped the lovely neck and arms,
The round white neck and snowy dimpled arms
Of Eithné; or, with heavy foot, awoke
A groan from Cairbré's armour on the wall—
A groan his sonless heart gave deeply back;
Or in the distance heard some damsel singing
A favourite song of Ailbhé's, and drew forth
Her golden hair and bathed it in his tears.

At last the king's high-ollamh thus began:
"O Cormac, son of Art and son of Conn
The hundred-battled, let our souls declare
What long hath lain a burthen on our peace.
We see thee seeming cheerful on the days
Of weekly wassail, chess, and race and chase,
Yet to the careful eye concealing grief:
We mark thee on the morns of law and judgment
Discreetly question and deliberate weave
Thy ordered thoughts in well-knit weighty speech.
Yet miss thee, as of old, on thy discourses
Broidering the opal flowers of eloquence,
Or flashing through them, to the listener's joy,
The diamond ray of reason-dazzling wit.
Nay, when that suitor seeking penalty
Exceeding great for satire on himself
So bitter true, that when big-bellied, bald
With blunder-breeding tongue, he raging rose
Before the Brehon who rehearsed the *rann*,
A shout of long, side-shaking laughter broke
From all the young at once, till here and there
Flashing a furious glance, the satirised
Retreated with his paunch toward thee, king,
Yet, careless of his trailing scabbard, tripped,
And backward staggering with blind hands in air

Caught thy chief cook by his long foxy beard
Behind the door, and fistful of red hair
Plumped howling on the pavement. Then ourselves,
The elders, might no more restrain the mirth
That swelled our cheeks to bursting. Out it blew
In bass so brazen or such bleating treble,
All laughed the louder save thyself alone,
Only one smile, one faintly flickering smile
Of dim December sunshine lit thy lips.
Now in the name of all thy loving people,
Princes and Lords and Commons, I am come
Beseeching thee that I may take the Branch
And shake it o'er thy head and so subdue
Thy grief with glamour, that the memory
Of all thine evil loss may from thy mind
Fade utterly, and again thou may'st arise
And take to wife the fairest, purest Princess
Wide-bordered Erin boasts, and sow anew
Seed-royal that shall richly round thee rise
Thy manhood's hope, thy flowering fence of age."

  Yet Cormac yielded not his people's prayer,
But root-fast in his barren grief endured,
Until the leaden-pacing year revolved
To the dark day that left him desolate.

Then he arose and thrust the Fairy Branch
Into his bosom and went forth alone
To that sad region where his Three had left him :
When straight a magic mist gathered and gloomed
Nor melted, till there smote upon his ear
The sound of manly voices sweetly singing
To harp and timpan touched with tuneful skill,
And look, a noble company of youths
With five slain harts and fifty wearied hounds
Beneath a mighty hunting-booth carousing
Upon the mountain. These with gracious greeting
Rising received him, and their chief approached,
And in an hospitable hand took his,
And led him to the seat of utmost honour
Beside him, and besought him to partake
Their banquet, ever host-like urging him
To each its choicest dainties. But the soul
Of Cormac craved no meats, tho' much he praised them,
And ever guest-like feigned an unfelt hunger :
Yet as they spake and jested, and sang and harped,
Scarce tasting food, he quaffed the circling cup,
Red with the grape and sweet with heather honey,
Until his heart grew merry and he forgat
The Fairy Branch ; then swift his host put forth
A secret hand to where it shook and sparkled

Within his bosom, when lo! the three gold apples
That hung the lowest of the nine rang forth
A tuneless warning, and the monarch caught
The robber's wrist, and wrung the bough therefrom.
And shook it o'er him and his company,
And forthwith they fell grovelling to the ground
In the similitude of filthy swine;
And Cormac knew that he had scarce escaped
The Cup of Cursing, that of the face of man,
Stamped with God's image, makes a bestial front,
And of the mouth, wherefrom His prayer and praise
Should chiefly flow—a monster's ravening maw.

Again a mist of magic gathering gloomed
Around the king, nor passed from off his path
Until a moon of harvest thrilled it through
With golden glimmering glory, and he was 'ware
Of one apparelled as a princess, crouched
Wild weeping on the earth, her reckless hands
Rending her radiant hair. And Cormac's heart
Was melted, and he asked her of her grief.
Then with bowed head she poured a lamentation
Of her young hero-lover fallen in fight.
And Cormac met her woe with words of solace,
And she took comfort and turned to him a face

Whiter than any swan upon the wave—
A form of fairer fashion. Then the king
Looked closelier at her, and with wonder viewed
Her yellow curls, clustering like rings of gold
Around her waist, and marked her tearful eyes
Dart through their dusky fringes a dewy beam
Bluer than ever evening's weeping star
Shed through the curtain of a summer's cloud:
When suddenly she oped them full on him
With wistful gaze, and as she looked a blush
Took her pale visage, while her slender hand
Stole throbbing into his. A mighty spell
Possessed his soul, and nearer still and nearer
He drew her, till he breathed her red lips' balm,
And passionately had pressed them to his own—
When lo! the midmost row of apples rang
The warning of the Branch, and in his breast
He caught the woman's thievish hand upon it,
And wrung it from her grasp, and o'er her head
Shook it, and of a sudden her soft, white palm
Shrivelled, her lovely apple-blossom cheeks
Withered away, her eyes of heavenly blue
Grew blear and evil, all her swan-like shape
Dwindled and shrank; till at the last there writhed
Whining before him a little crook-back witch.

Once more the magic mist obscured his course,
Nor passed until the sun with purple beam
Piercing its cloud displayed a goodly group
Of sages seated, all with eager speech
In such dispute, none knew or seemed to know
Cormac had joined him to their company,
Until an end was made to their discourse
Sophistical of love and life and death.
Then with a courteous welcome they inquired
His mind upon their thoughts, and led him on,
Lauding his judgment, gravely to propound
And keenly argue; till at last he grew
So soul-enamoured of their sophistries
That when the sage in chief with flattering tongue
Besought him bide with them continually—
Such need, such heavy need had they of one
In wit so shrewd, in eloquence so lofty—
He fain had fared with them, but ere he spoke,
The young Branch-bearer's words came back to him:
" *Well hast thou kept thy promise; wherefore take
A blessing for thy truth's sake—aye, a blessing
Shall win thee victory,*" while a tuneless peal
Rang from the topmost row of golden apples
Upon the Fairy Bough, and Cormac caught
The elder's thievish hand within his bosom

Upon the Branch, and wrung it fiercely from him,
And shook it o'er him and his sophist crew,
And lo! they vanished gibbering before him,
A grinning troop of fleshless skeletons.

Again the King of Erin went his ways,
Nor now had been long journeying, when there stretched
An hundred-acred field before him, bright
With stooks of golden corn; three spear-casts further,
Crowning a sudden, green, far-looking mound,
A mansion, many windowed, sunset-flattered
To topaz, ruby, amethyst, shone and sparkled
A thousand welcomes, while, behind, a forest
Laughed back all emerald. Through the field of corn
He swiftly strode, with noble heart presaging
His goal at last, and climbed the hill and sought
The mansion, took the hand-log in his hand
And boldly knocked. Immediate to the wall
The door sprang open of its own accord,
While from within a mighty summons came,
"In God's name, enter!" Straight he entered in,
Following the voice, and reached a royal hall,
Huge, black-oak-raftered, silver-pillared, hung
Its circuit through with brightly burnished arms,

Elk-antlers, giant boar-tusks, jewelled beakers—
By seven great archways pierced, with couches seven,
Silk canopied, yew-carven, fine-fur-covered,
Betwixt each twain; a royal champion's seat
Of beaten gold before its blazing hearth,
And on the seat a princely Chieftain, clad
In many-coloured raiment, at his side
A bright apparelled Princess.

      These arose
At Cormac's coming, and bespake him thus:
"Whoe'er thou art, oh Stranger, 'tis no hour
To further fare on foot, seeing the sun
Is well-nigh set; then sit thee down with us
And share our banquet, and abide the night
Beneath our roof, till rosy morn return."
Then Cormac, son of Art, sat gladly down.

 "Go forth now to the grove," the woman cried.
"Oh goodman of the house; thy spear in hand,
For lo! there lacks sufficiency of meat
To sate our want." Therewith the chief arose,
His hunting spear in hand, and fared abroad,
Nor tarried long without; but soon returned,
A great wood-ranging, acorn-crushing boar,
Fresh skinned and cleaned and quartered, on his back.
And in his hand a mighty log of pine,

And cast them down before the fire; and thus
To Cormac and the Princess smiling spake:
"There have ye meat, now cook it for yourselves."
"After what manner?" asked the son of Art.
"That I will teach thee," saith his host; "Arise,
And make four quarters of this log of pine,
Then lay a quarter log upon the fire,
And o'er it one full quarter of the boar,
And tell a tale of truth, however short,
Above it, and that quarter shall be roast."

Then Cormac rose and caught a glittering axe,
And proved it keen and true, and eyed the wood,
And stepping backwards swung the biting steel
Once from his shoulder, and the great log fell
Clean cleft in twain; twice, thrice, and smote in half
Each equal portion.

                Next the woman laid
A quarter faggot on the leaping fire,
And o'er it one full quarter of the swine.

Then Cormac spake: "Since each hath borne his part,
'Twere ill-befitting that the one, a guest,
Should further tell a tale of truth for two—
His host and hostess." "Right thou art, forsooth,"
The prince replied. "And now methinks thy speech,
Matched with thy noble mien, bewrays thee royal;

Therefore my story first.
                        That boar is one
Of seven, yet could I feed the world with them;
For I have but to take his bones abroad,
And bury them beneath a sacred tree,
And, look, the sod begins to sway and surge,
Till sudden, from his scarce dug sepulchre,
The monstrous beast breaks bellowing away."

   That tale was true; and lo! the flesh was roast.
"Tell now thy tale, fair princess," saith the king.
"I will," quoth she, "but do thou first lay down
Thy quarter log upon the leaping fire,
And o'er it one full quarter of the boar."
So it was done.
                "Seven cows are mine," saith she,
"Snow white from horn to hoof, and not a day
Dawns or declines but these with matchless milk
Fill seven full kieves, and here's my hand to you,
My kine could milk enough to satisfy
The souls of all the sons of earth assembled
Athirst on yonder plain."
                        That tale was true.
And lo! her quarter of the boar was roast.
   Then Cormac: "If thy tale be true indeed
Thy husband there is Mananan, thyself

His wedded wife; for on the face of earth
Exists there not the owner of such treasures
Save Mananan alone, for to Tir Tairrngire
He went to seek thy hand and won it well,
And therewithal to dower, these wondrous cows,
And coughed upon them till he quite constrained
Their udders to his will."

"Full wisely now
Hast thou divined us both!" cried Mananan.
"But tell a story for thy quarter now."
"Ay! sure," saith Cormac, "yet do thou lay down
Thy faggot now upon the leaping fire,
And over it thy quarter of the swine."
So it was done, and thus the King outspake:
"I come, indeed, upon an anxious quest,
For 'tis the year to-day my wife and son
And daughter, three most dear on earth to me,
Were borne afar." "By whom?" asked Mananan.
"A youth," the King replied, "there came to me,
Bearing a golden branch, for which my heart
Conceived so deep desire, I granted him
The full award of his own mouth for it,
The which he thus pronounced against my peace:
'Therefore I claim thy wife, thy son, thy daughter,—
Chaste Eithné, gallant Cairbré, winsome Ailbhé.'"

"If what thou sayest be true," cried Mananan,
"Thyself art Cormac, son of Art, the son
Of hundred-battled Conn." "That same am I,"
Quoth Cormac, "and in quest of these I come."
That tale was true, and lo! his quarter roast.

"Eat now thy meat," bespake him Mananan.
"I never yet broke bread," the King replied,
"Having two only in my company."
"Would'st thou consume it with three more, O Cormac?"
"Yea, good mine host, were they but dear to me."
Then Mananan arose and oped the door,
The farthest from his hearth, and straight led in
Chaste Eithné, gallant Cairbré, winsome Ailbhé,
And these in utter rapture around him clinging
The King embraced with tears and sobs of joy.

Thereafter Cormac and his queen and children
Sat down to meat, and on the festal board
A table-cloth of snowy silk was spread.
"'Tis a full precious thing thou see'st before thee,
O Cormac, son of Art," saith Mananan;
"For never yet was food so delicate
But thrice demanded of this charmèd cloth
Straight stands thereon." "Nay, that indeed is well,"

Quoth Cormac. Then the other smiling thrust
His hand into his girdle and drew forth
A golden cup and set it on his palm.
"A magic marvel is this cup of mine,
Seeing no drink can be desired therefrom
But look, the same leaps bubbling to its brim!"
"That too is well, O Mananan!" "Moreover,
'Tis of the virtues of this magic cup
That when a lying tale is told before it,
Lo! it lies broken. Tell a tale of truth,
And on the instant it is whole again."
"Let that be proved, O Mananan!" "Then give ear,
O Cormac! This thy wife I bore from thee
In sooth hath had another husband since."
Therewith in pieces lay the fairy cup.
"A lying tale!" his princess answered him;
"Nor man nor woman hath she seen, save us
And these her children dear." That tale was true,
And straight the fairy cup was whole again.
 "Priceless possessions verily are these,
O Mananan," saith Cormac. "Thine henceforth,
Two precious tokens, Cormac, of my friendship,
To wit, the charmèd cloth and magic cup;
The Fairy Branch, moreover, treasure still.
And now the banquet waits us, and believe

That hadst thou here an host in multitude
Not one should miss of hospitable cheer.
And in this cup I pledge thee, for I searched
Thine inmost soul with spells, that thou and these
Might share this joyful feast of fellowship."

   Thereafterward they supped right royally ;
For not a meat they thought on but that cloth
Forthwith displayed, nor any drink desired
But straight it sparkled in that magic cup.
And for that fairy feast to Mananan
The Four gave thanks exceeding, and arose
And bade their Hosts good night, and laid them down
On kingly couches richly strewn for them,
And swiftly fell on slumber and sweet sleep,
And where they woke upon the morrow morn
Was in their pleasant palace Liathdrum.

BELTANE.

(*See* Notes.)

Oh, mild May day, in Fōdla's clime
Of fairy colour, the laughing prime
Of leafy summer from year to year,
I would that Leagha were with me here
To lie and listen down in a dell
To Banba's blackbirds warbling well,
And her cuckoos crying with constant strain
Welcome, welcome the bright Beltane;
When the swallows are skimming the shore,
    And the swift steed stoops to the fountain,
And the weak, fair bog-down grows on the moor,
    And the heath spreads her hair on the mountain,
And the signs of heaven are in consternation,
    And the rushing planets such radiance pour,
That the sea lies lulled, and the generation
    Of flowers awakes once more.

PATRICK AND OISIN.

(See Notes.)

"Oisin, Oisin, too long is thy slumber.
  Oisin, arise, and give ear to the chant :
  Thy force hath forsook thee, thy battles are over,
  And without us, old man, thou would'st perish of want."

"My force hath forsook me, my battles are over :
  Since alas the famed empire of Finn is no more,
  And without you indeed 'tis for want I should perish,
  But since Finn sweetest music is music no more."

"Nay, silly old man, for all of thy vaunting,
  Of the loud Dord-Finn chorus, the timpan and horn,
  Thou hast never heard music like matin bells ringing,
  Or solemn psalms sung in the still summer morn."

"Though greatly thou praisest the chants of the clerics,
  I had rather lie listening down in the dale
  To the voice of the cuckoo of Letter Lee calling ;
  Or the very sweet thrushes of green Gleann-a-Sgail ;

"Or the song of the blackbird of Derrycarn gushing
　So full and so free in the woods of the West;
　(Oh, Patrick, no hymn under heaven could approach it!
　Ah, would that I only were under his nest!)

"And I'd far liefer hearken the eagle's fierce whistle,
　From lone Glennamoo or the Ridge by the stream,
　Or list the loud thunder of rushing Tra-Rury,
　Or catch on rough Irrus the seagull's scream.

"And I'd bid long goodbye to the bells of the clerics,
　Could I once again follow o'er mountain and moor
　The tune of the twelve fleetest wolf hounds of Erin
　Let loose with their faces away from the Suir.

"And Cnu, little Cnu of my bosom, where art thou?
　O small fairy dwarf, to the Finians so dear,
　Whose harp ever soothed all our sorrows to slumber,
　Ah, Cnu, little Cnu, how I would you were here.

"Where is now your betrothed one, oh, Cnu, where is Blathnaid,
　Who stood up in beauty to sing when you played;
　For the mouth of no mortal such sweetness could utter,
　As the soft, rosy mouth of that magical maid."

CUCULLAIN'S LAMENT OVER FERDIAH.

Oh, mightiest of the host of Maev,
   Ferdiah, sweetest mouth of song,
   Heroic arm most swift and strong
To slaughter or to save.

O curls, O softly rustling wreath
   Of yellow curls that round him rolled,
   One beauteous belt of glistering gold,—
Who laid you low in death?

Blue eyes that beamed with friendship bright
   Upon me through the battle press,
   Or o'er the mimic field of chess,—
Who quenched your kingly light?

Alas, Ferdiah, overthrown
   By this red hand at last you fell!
   My bosom's brother, was it well?
Ochone, ochone, ochone!

THE SONG OF THE FAIRY KING.

Queen of women, oh come away,
    Come to my kingdom strange to see;
Where tresses flow with a golden glow,
    And white as snow is the fair body.

Under the arching of ebon brows,
    Eyes of azure the soul enthral,
And a speech of songs to the mouth belongs,
    And sorrowful sighing shall ne'er befall.

Bright are the blooms of Innisfail,
    Green her forests wave in the west:
But brighter flowers and greener bowers
    Shall all be ours in that country blest.

Can her streams compare to the runnels rare
    Of yellow honey and rosy wine
That softly slip to the longing lip
    With magic flow through that land of mine?

We roam the earth in its grief and mirth,
    But move unseen of all therein,
For before their gaze there hangs a haze,
    The heavy haze of their mortal sin.

But our age wastes not, our beauty tastes not
    Evil's apple nor droops nor dies;
Death slays us never, but love for ever
    With stainless ardour illumes our eyes.

Then, queen of women, oh come away,
    Come and sit on my fairy throne,
In a realm of rest with spirits blest,
    Where sin and sorrow are all unknown.

O'CURNAN'S SONG.

O Mary bhan asthore,
That through my bosom's core
Hast pierced me past the Isle of Fōdla's healing;
By Heaven, 'tis my belief,
Had you but known my grief,
Long since to me with succour you'd been stealing.

With tears the night I waste;
No food by day I taste,
But wander weak and silent as a shadow!
Ah! if I may not find
My Mary true and kind,
My mother soon must weep, a sonless widow.

I know not night from day:
"Cuckoo!" the thrushes say!
But how can it be May in dark December?
My friends look strange and wild;
But hasten, Mary mild,
And well my heart its mistress shall remember.

No herb or skill of hand
My cure can now command,
From you, O Flower of Love, alone I'll seek it;
Then hasten, hasten here,
My own and only dear,
And in your secret ear I'll softly speak it.

One sweet kiss from your mouth
Would quench my burning drouth,
And lift me back to life; ah! yield it to me;
Or make for me my bed
Among the mouldering dead,
Where the winding worms may crawl and channel through me.

Ah! better buried so
Than like a ghost to go,
All music, dance, and sport with sighs forsaking;
A witless, wandering man
For the love of Mary bhan,
With the heart within my bosom slowly breaking.

CAOINE.

Cold, dark, and dumb lies my boy on his bed;
Cold, dark, and silent the night dews are shed;
Hot, swift, and fierce fall my tears for the dead!

His footprints lay light in the dew of the dawn
As the straight, slender track of the young mountain fawn;
But I'll ne'er again follow them over the lawn.

His manly cheek blushed with the sun's rising ray,
And he shone in his strength like the sun at midday;
But a cloud of black darkness has hid him away.

And that black cloud for ever shall cling to the skies:
And never, ah, never, I'll see him arise,
Lost warmth of my bosom, lost light of my eyes!

SONGS AND SKETCHES.

SONG.

Some go smiling through the grey time.
  Under naked, songless bowers:
Some go mourning all the May time,
  'Mid the laughing leaves and flowers.
      Why is this,
        Rosy Bliss
    Comes to kiss Winter grey?
      Why, ah! why
        Doth Sorrow sigh
    On the lap of lovely May?

Happy Love, with song and smiling,
  Through the withered woodland goes:
Hapless Love hath no beguiling
  From the redbreast or the rose.
      This is why
        Woods may sigh,

Flowers die and hearts be gay:
This, alas!
The piteous pass
That leaves us mourning all the May.

FROM THE RED ROSE.

From the red rose to the apple-blossom,
    From the apple-blossom to the blue sky,
Looking up still in the spring-tide,
    When none else is by,
        For a love born
        On a May morn,
Long, long ago, I sigh.

From the blue sky to the apple-blossom,
    And the roses in row,
Looking down still in the spring-tide,
    Through my garden I go,
        For a love lost
        In a spring frost,
Singing Heigh ho, heigh ho!

O BRANCH OF FRAGRANT BLOSSOM.

O BRANCH of fragrant blossom,
  How the heart in my bosom
Lay heaving before you with hopeless sigh;
  Till your voice grew low and tender,
  And a soft, love-lit splendour
Shone out to save me from your dark, dreamy eye.

O branch of rosy blossom,
  Radiant bride of my bosom,
My heart heaves no longer with hopeless sigh;
  For you 're the blessed shadow
  Upon my burning meadow,
My sunshine in winter, and my love till I die.

ONE LOVING SMILE.

O, WHITE and red,
Above your head
The arbutus flowers and berries grow;
And underneath
The blushing heath
I've found for luck the heath of snow;
And sure 'tis fine
The foamy line
That laughs across the purple bay;
But, ah, let slip
From your ripe lip
One loving smile, and where are they?

SNOW DRIFT.

Sigh on, sad wind,
    O'er hill and forest,
With thee my spirit
    Would fain go forth :
Thus unconfined,
    When grief was sorest,
I should inherit
    The dreary north.

With thee I'd sail
    On viewless pinion
O'er snowy spaces
    Where man is not ;
And all things wail
    The frost's dominion,
And summer's graces
    Are all forgot.

For my great grief,
    All solace scorning,

Abhors the heaven
   She's left a hell:
O'er flower and leaf,
   The purple morning,
The golden even,
   She spreads a spell.

Till human speech
   Seems false and hollow--
In man and woman
   God's image lost.
Then I beseech
   That I may follow
To haunts inhuman
   Of snow and frost.

More true and chaste,
   Thou bitter Norland,
Than southern languor,
   Hot-blooded jars;
Thy wintry waste,
   Thy solemn foreland,
Aurora's anger
   Amongst the stars.

Sigh on, sad wind.
  O'er hill and forest,
With thee my spirit
  Would fain go forth;
Thus unconfined,
  When grief was sorest,
I should inherit
  The dreary north.

SHAMROCK LEAVES.

Oh ! if for every tear
   That from our exiled eyes
Has fallen, Erin dear,
   A shamrock could arise,
We'd weave a garland green
   Should stretch the ocean through,
All, all the way between
   Our aching hearts and you !

SNOW STAINS.

The snow had fallen, and fallen from heaven,
    Unnoticed in the night,
As o'er the sleeping sons of God
    Floated the manna white;
And still though small flowers crystalline
    Blanched all the earth beneath,
Angels with busy hands above
    Renewed the airy wreath;
When, white amid the falling flakes,
    And fairer far than they,
Beside her wintry casement hoar
    A dying woman lay.
"More pure than yonder virgin snow
    From God comes gently down
I left my happy country home,"
    She sighed, "to seek the town.
More foul than yonder drift shall turn,
    Before the sun is high,
Down-trodden and defiled of men,
    More foul," she wept, "am I.

Yet, as in midday might confessed,
   Thy good sun's face of fire
Draws the chaste spirit of the snow
   To meet him from the mire,
Lord, from this leprous life in death
   Lift me, Thy Magdalene,
That rapt into Redeeming Light
   I may once more be clean."

A SONG OF THE SEASONS.

  Oh! the Spring's delight
  Is the cowslip bright,
As she laughs to the warbling linnet,
  And a whistling thrush
  On a white May bush,
And his mate on her nest within it.

  Summer she shows
  Her rose, her rose!
And oh! all the happy night long
  The nightingale woos her;
  At dawn the lark sues her,
With the crystal surprise of his song.

  King Autumn's crown
  Is the barley brown,
Red over with rosy fruit;
  And the yellow trees,
  As they sigh in the breeze,
Are the strings of his solemn lute.

Old Winter's breath
Is cold as death,
'Tis lonesome he's left the earth;
Yet the thrush he sings,
And the rose she springs
From the flame of his fairy hearth.

MAUREEN.

Blue eyes 'mid ebon lashes lost,
Gold hair o'er silver shoulders tossed,
Lips crimson coral ivory-crossed—
    Maureen!

To-day to confidence beguiled;
To-morrow haughty, wayward, wild;
A woman half and half a child—
    Maureen.

SPRING'S SECRETS.

As once I paused on poet wing
    In the green heart of a grove,
I met the Spirit of the Spring,
    With her great eyes lit of Love.

She took me gently by the hand,
    And whispered in my anxious ear
Secrets none may understand,
    Till she make their meaning clear:

" Why the primrose looks so pale;
    Why the rose is set with thorns;
Why the magic nightingale
    Through the darkness mourns and mourns."

She ceased: a leafy murmur sighed
    Softly through the listening trees.
Anon she uttered, eager-eyed,
    These her joyful mysteries:

"How the angels, as they pass
 With their vesture pure and white
O'er the shadowy garden grass,
 Touch the lilies into light:

"Or with hidden hands of love
 Guide the throstle's wavering wings,
But show their faces bright above,
 Only where the skylark sings."

THE REJECTED LOVER.

On Innisfallen's fairy isle,
    Amid the blooming bushes,
We leant upon the lover's stile,
    And listened to the thrushes;
When first I sighed to see her smile,
    And smiled to see her blushes.

Her hair was bright as beaten gold,
    And soft as spider's spinning;
Her cheek out-bloomed the apple old
    That set our parents sinning;
And in her eyes you might behold
    My joys and griefs beginning.

In Innisfallen's fairy grove
    I hushed my happy wooing,
To listen to the brooding dove
    Amid the branches cooing;
But oh! how short those hours of love,
    How long their bitter rueing!

Poor cushat thy complaining breast
 With woe like mine is heaving;
With thee I mourn a fruitless quest,
 For ah! with art deceiving,
The cuckoo-bird has robbed my nest,
 And left me wildly grieving.

THE BEAUTIFUL BAY.

(A CADENCE OF KENMARE RIVER.)

I LIFTED mine eyes and beheld him lying, that Harper old, on the green sea-grass,
And I said in my heart, "I will rise and seek a lonelier spot, O mother dear;
For this thy sea and these thy woods, and those thy violet hills and vales,
At the coming of others, estrange from my soul all their low, sweet communings."
So I arose. Now he spake no word, but he glanced a glance, and his spirit met mine,
And swifter than speech, and surer far, thus he answered my secret thought.
"Avoid not! I hush not her rich revealings, for I am hers, aye, even as thou;
Avoid not, for surely she drew us together, her dearest children, for only this,—
To breathe to us both some tenderer tidings than ever she whispered each soul apart."

I looked in his face, and I believed the eloquent blue of
    the old man's eye,
And I knew, by the ruddy rose of his cheek, and the full,
    white flower of his flowing hair,
A son, indeed, of Nature's love. I looked, and I loved
    him for her sake,
And returned again to my seat in silence, and side by side
    on the soft sea-grass,
With the bluest blue of heaven above us, we sat at gaze
    on the Beautiful Bay.
Gazing, gazing, oh delight! for the sea-turn blew from the
    ocean beyond,
And ever before his full, sweet voice the Arbutus Islands,
    for utter joy,
Shivered in every sparkling leaf, and called, "He comes!"
    to the wooing waves.
And these leaped back with a silver laugh, and cried it to
    all of their crystal clan,
And the white smile spread, and hither and thither, with
    dark, swift fingers pointed to shore
The wind-flaws darted o'er the dreaming azure, and the
    ripples danced after in a diamond dance,
And nearer and nearer the rapture ran, till the cool air
    kissed on the craving cheek.

O breathing balm! O sweet sea-spice! O wind of the west, that most I love!

Now the Sea had risen, and wrestled and lost and wrestled and won with the struggling Shore

For the golden spoils they win and lose with the Moon above for arbitress;

'Till only one thin, red torque remained for Ocean's triumphant conquesting.

Then the sea-turn fluttered with fainting wings, fluttered, fluttered, failed, and fell;

And the Sun strode down from mountain to mountain, kissing their foreheads with his farewell kiss

To a happy rose that flushed through heaven, and thrilled and trembled out of sight.

Then the sweet night fell, and the soft stars shone, and we sang, "Good night!" to the Beautiful Bay.

AMBROSE AND UNA.

It was the good Sir Ambrose
　　Came spurring to the sea,
And to woo the beauteous Una
　　From his castle high rode he.

They plighted their troth together,
　　And sealed it with seals of gold,
But a month and a day thereafter
　　The good knight slept in the mould.

Now, alas! for the Lady Una,
　　She made such bitter moan
That the dead Sir Ambrose heard her
　　From his grave in the churchyard lone.

Up rose the dead Sir Ambrose,
　　All in his shroud of white,
And to his true love's bower
　　Stole softly through the night.

He tapped at his true love's bower,
    With his hand so long and thin;
"I pray thee, dearest Una,
    Let thy loving bridegroom in."

But his dear lady answered,
    "I cannot ope the door
Till Jesu's name thou namest,
    As thou wast wont before."

"Rise, oh! rise, dear Una,
    Nor fear to unbar the door;
I can name the blessed Jesu
    As I was wont before."

Up rose the weeping Una,
    And her bower opened wide,
And the dead Sir Ambrose entered
    And sat by her bedside.

With her golden comb his true love
    Combed out his tresses dear,
And each fair lock, as she kissed it,
    She bathed with the bitter tear.

And "Oh! tell me, dearest Ambrose,
    By thy Una's love," she said,
"How fares it since they laid thee
    In thy dark and lonesome bed?"

"Whenever thy sorrow, Una,
    Is soothed in sacred prayer,
Forthwith my gloomy coffin
    Is filled with roses fair.

"But whenever, oh! my Una,
    Thy grief is wild and loud,
Those soft and fragrant roses
    Turn to tears upon my shroud.

"Dost hear the red cock crowing?
    I must no longer stay;
'Tis the hour the churchyard claims us,
    The sad hour before the day."

So the good Sir Ambrose turned him,
    Deep sighing from the door,
And to the lonely churchyard
    Went silently once more.

But Una followed after,
    And clasped her true love's hand,
And forth they fared together
    To the dark and dreadful land.

They could not speak for sorrow;
    The grave too soon was nigh;
And Sir Ambrose' fair hair faded
    As flames to ashes die.

Till, as they stood together,
    Where the dead man's tomb was made,
Whilst his cheeks grew wan and hollow,
    Sir Ambrose faintly said:

"Look up to the sky, my Una,
    For my moments swiftly fail;
Look up and tell me truly
    Is this the dawning pale?"

She turned her sad face from him
    Toward the coming light,
When straight the good Sir Ambrose
    Softly melted from her sight.

To her bower went poor Una,
    And prayed to Jesu blest,
That ere the year was over
    She, too, might be at rest.

But the month and the day thereafter
    Upon her bier she lay,
And now, with good Sir Ambrose,
    Awaits the Judgment Day.

ORPHEUS TO PLUTO.

OH Thou, whom alone of Immortals
    But to name is a fear among men,
Through the gloom of whose terrible portals
    Is no turning again,
When, ghost after ghost, to thy regions
    Unlovely to flee we are fain,
As the wild winter-swans flock in legions
    Remote o'er the main!

I come not with insult Titanic
    To thy consort as Tityos came,
Whom to Lust, a perpetual panic,
    Thy retributive flame
At her feet laid immense in his anguish;
    Nor clothed on with Herakles' might,
Am I here thy Three-headed to vanquish,
    Dread Monarch of Night!

I, alas, am that Orpheus ill-fortuned,
    Who with song, in his pleasant youth flown,
Wooed flowers from waste places, importuned
    Clear streams from the stone;
And with magic maturer united
    Man to man in the graces of art,
Till Eros drew bow, and delighted
    Two souls with his smart.

Spring sisterly smiled on my wooing,
    Summer motherly welcomed my wife;
But a foe, Autumn entered, subduing
    All sweetness of life.
For alas, like a pure lily-blossom
    Transfixed by the brier of the brake,
She has fallen, the bride of my bosom,
    A spoil to the snake—

Evil beast, that for slaughter lay slunken
    Subtle-eyed at the shadowy ford,
What time, scarce escaped from the drunken
    Unchaste Honey-Lord,
Up the slope of the Hebrus she hurried,
    Witless quite of a new foe beneath,

Till his fangs in her fair flesh he buried—
    The darter of Death.

Grief-distraught by her side on the morrow,
    With rent raiment and locks dust-defiled,
Low I lay, till there stole on my sorrow
    The voice of a child.
"Take comfort, sad son of Apollo!
    Arise, nothing fearing, and lay
Thy hand to thy lute-strings, and follow,
    For Love leads the way."

From the corse my despairful clasp sunders;
    Hope-flushed the dear harp I invade;
Earth shakes at the sound, the air thunders,
    And the deeps are dismayed.
Yea! the Day Sire above thee, thy brother,
    Tellus old, and the Lord of the Main,
Weird laughter with strange sighings smother,
    Mirth with moanings of pain;

Whilst a God to thine awful dominion
    Greatly guided my feet from above,
The All-wise, All-pervasive-of-pinion,
    Omnipotent Love!

On we fared! Orcus opened to list us!
    On we fared! Death herself dropped a tear!
Charon, Cerberus, may not resist us,
    And unharmed we are here.

Now, O King, for the cause of our mission
    Thou hast heard; knowing also the worth
Of the lost one, at Love's own petition
    Redeem her to earth!—
Love, who steered thy black steeds to the meadows
    Of Enna, and won thee the bride,
Who now queens it o'er congregate shadows,
    Enthroned at thy side!—
Love, the ally, through whom thou prolongest
    Bliss supreme in these joyless abodes!
Love! Love! still the weakest, the strongest,
    Eldest, youngest of Gods!

SONG: TO E. P.

When our little Queen was born,
    Winter first with furious pother
Flew to fix his icy scorn
    On the infant and the mother.

But in such a loving fashion
    Side by side he found them laid,
That to pity all his passion
    Melting quite, he softly said:

"Child and mother sleep unharmed!
    See how vanquished by your beauty
Winter's dreadful self disarmed
    Kneels to do you dearest duty."

Then a courser blast bestriding,
    Winter waved his wild adieu,
And the gentle spring came guiding
    To the couch her zephyrs blue.

Leaning there, the imperial maid,
    From the crystal car that bore her,
Lightly her flower-sceptre laid
    On the lovely babe before her,

Whisp'ring, "Since thy wiles have driven
    Winter from my budding bowers,
Every grace I e'er have given,
    Mortal maiden, shall be yours.

"See! I touch with violets two
    Lisa's lids, in token tender
Of the eyes of modest blue
    That shall most enchantment lend her.

"Next I lay these mountain daisies,
    Clustering close with crimson tips
Round their petals' pearly graces,
    For a sign on Lisa's lips.

"Now her tiny cheek I tint
    With this trailing apple blossom,
And these snowdrops for a hint
    Drop into her dainty bosom.

"Last for Lisa's heart this pansy!"
    Here she stooped and whispering spoke.
    Ere she sped, so fond a fancy
        That our Lisa smiling woke.

CHOOSING A PROFESSION.

"When Robin's a big man, what will wee Robin be?"
So he peeped, half afraid,
From the cozy little nest that in mother's gown he'd made,
Our plump, rosy Robin, he peeped out and said :
"A sailor I will be,
To sail upon the sea,
But papa and mamma, won't you sail along with me?"

"No! the captain of the ship wouldn't let mamma sail,
He'd only take me."
"Then oh! what a cruel man the captain must be,
Not to take my dear mamma to sail upon the sea.
So, papa, I'll be instead,
A soldier all in red,
With a sword in my hand and a helmet on my head—

"And I'll fight, fight, fight, for papa and for mamma."
"But if you were killed?"   "Then I'd fly
Far away above the clouds O, so, so high,
Till I came to our Father on his throne in the sky.
And ask to be instead
Of a soldier all in red,
An angel all in white to keep watch beside your bed."

MYRTILLA.

Myrtilla boasts a marble brow
   By ebon tresses softly swept,
Myrtilla's mouth is Cupid's bow
   In rosy nectar newly dipped,
And heaven's own azure lights her eyes,
   Her cheek bids roses blush in vain;
Say, shall the lovely nymph surprise
   This bosom with her conquering chain?

Nay, I mistrust the studied skill
   That twines her tresses' silken snare;
The honied sigh her lips distil
   Is heaved with too consummate care;
Her eyes, with all too amorous art,
   Now shun, and now upon me shine;
Too well thou hast rehearsed thy part,
   Myrtilla, ever to be mine!

LOVE'S SURPRISE.

He sang as he lay on Mangerton mountain,
    That Irish knight who had never known love.
"What song so sweet as the chiming fountain?
    What blue so blue as the heaven above?"
Fond heart! for nearer and nearer drew
A sweeter voice and an eye more blue.

"O what can blush by the purple heather?
    What gold with the gorse-flower dare compare?"
He turned, fond heart, and found them together,
    On her glowing cheek and her glittering hair.
Now what for the knight are the hill-flower's dyes,
The fountain's voice and the sapphire skies?

She had lost her path, that lovely lady,
    Whose heart had never a lord confessed;
O bright she blushed, and gently prayed he
    Would guide her over the mountain crest;
And little loth was the gallant knight
To squire the steps of that lady bright.

So he took her hand, and they passed together,
  The knight and the lady unlearned of love,
Through the golden gorse and the purple heather—
  O laughingly beamed the blue above,
And the fountain sang as their feet went by,
The sibyl fountain, "*For aye, for aye.*"

AMŒBÆAN.

HE.

THE sky has lost the happy lustre
   It borrowed from her azure eyes,
The unruly winds around me bluster,
   Unsoftened by her balmy sighs,
And for my true love's loss alone
The thronging town's a desert grown.

SHE.

Along the glen and o'er the heather,
   With spring's return once more I stray
Through scenes where oft we've roved together
   At rosy dawn and gloaming grey;
But all these former haunts of bliss,
Love, without thee their beauty miss!

HE.

By arch triumphal, lordly tower,
   With thoughts like these I soothe my way—

"What sculptured flower could match her bower
　　With wreaths of living roses gay?
And piles superb, and courtly hall,
　　For her sweet cot I'd change you all."

She.

Now blooms each freshest, fairest blossom,
　　By woodland wild and garden wall,
Yet pressed unto this aching bosom,
　　These faint blue stars are worth them all.
For being too sad to speak the thought,
With these he sighed, "Forget me not."

He.

In art supreme, around us, o'er us,
　　Sweet Southern voices rise and float,
Or swells sublime the lofty chorus,
　　Or dies on one voluptuous note—
But how can mimic transports move,
After her unfeigned words of love?

She.

Let skylarks spring to meet the morrow
　　With lays of jubilant delight,

And Philomela's voice of sorrow
   Most passionate plead the livelong night:
If of sweet music I have choice,
Waft me one echo of his voice.

He.

Oh! what are city pomp and pride,
If Celia be not by my side?

She.

Oh! would that I my way might win
To that sweet town he sojourns in!

LOVE'S SONG.

Love is a boundless bliss:
    All they who share it
With lover's look and lover's kiss,
    Surely shall declare it.

Love is a precious pain:
    No skill can heal it,
When they who sigh but sigh in vain
    In their hearts conceal it.

Love with the crown of life
    His king and queen covers,
When gallant man and gentle wife
    Still are steadfast lovers.

Ah! and when envious Death
    One life shall smother,
Love with his willow-wreath
    Crowns that constant other.

Young men and maids, for love
   Seek, till ye find it,
And having found, win Heaven above
   About your hearts to bind it.

COMPANIONS.

Smile farewell to Sorrow:
Give to Joy good-morrow:
And charge him to continue
A quiet reign within you.

Smile farewell to Gladness,
Take the hand of Sadness,
And wistfully beseech her
To be your tender teacher.

So shall both befriend you,
And to the grave attend you;
There Sorrow from you sever,
Joy go with you ever.

GOOD NIGHT.

Good night! good night! our feast is ended,
By young and old with smiles attended;
Where Wit and Worth and Beauty blended,
  To speed the hours with dance and song.
      Beauty's smile
      Free from guile,
      Wit that shone
      Wounding none:
And manly Worth and Woman true,
Good night! and joy go home with you.

Good night! and may your minstrel's numbers
Still echo on amid your slumbers,
To spell-bind every care that cumbers
  The lover's heart, the mother's breast.
      Beauty, Mirth,
      Wit and Worth

Fall to sleep
Calm and deep,
Nor rouse, till rosy Morrow call,
"Awake, and joy go with you all!"

MUSIC

NOTE.

Of the following Irish airs only those specified in the Notes at the end of this volume have been harmonised and published as songs to my words.

Allowance should therefore be made in the case of the other poems in the Musical Appendix, which, though occasionally altered to suit the music better, doubtless, here and there require some further modification for the purposes of modern vocalisation.

A. P. G.

THE LITTLE RED LARK.

Oh, swan of slenderness,
Dove of tenderness,
  Jewel of joys, arise!
The little red lark
Like a rosy spark
  Of song to his sunburst flies.
But till thou art risen
Earth is a prison
  Full of my lonesome sighs;
Then awake and discover
To thy fond lover
  The morn of thy matchless eyes!

The dawn is dark to me;
Hark! oh, hark to me,
  Pulse of my heart, I pray!
And out of thy hiding
With blushes gliding,
  Dazzle me with thy day.
Ah, then, once more to thee
Flying I'll pour to thee
  Passion so sweet and gay,
The lark shall listen,
And dewdrops glisten,
  Laughing on every spray.

LOVE'S WISHES.

Would I were Erin's apple-blossom o'er you,
  Or Erin's rose in all its beauty blown,
To drop my richest petals down before you,
  Within the garden where you walk alone;
In hope you'd turn and pluck a little posy,
  With loving fingers through my foliage pressed,
And kiss it close and set it blushing rosy
  To sigh out all its sweetness on your breast.

Would I might take the pigeon's flight towards you,
  And perch beside your window-pane above,
And murmur how my heart of hearts it hoards you,
  O hundred thousand treasures of my love;
In hope you'd stretch your slender hand and take me,
  And smooth my wildly-fluttering wings to rest,
And lift me to your loving lips and make me
  My bower of blisses in your loving breast.

I ONCE LOVED A BOY.

I once loved a boy, and a bold Irish boy,
  Far away in the hills of the West;
Ah! the love of that boy was my jewel of joy,
  And I built him a bower in my breast,
    In my breast;
  And I built him a bower in my breast.

I once loved a boy, and I trusted him true,
  And I built him a bower in my breast;
But away, wirrasthrue! the rover he flew,
  And robbed my poor heart of its rest,
    Of its rest;
  And robbed my poor heart of its rest.

The spring-time returns, and the sweet speckled thrush
  Murmurs soft to his mate on her nest,
But for ever there's fallen a sorrowful hush
  O'er the bower that I built in my breast,
    In my breast;
  O'er the desolate bower in my breast.

HUSH SONG.

I would hush my lovely laddo,
In the green arbutus' shadow,
O'er the fragrant, flowering meadow,
    In the smiling spring-time.
        Shoheen sho lo, Shoheen hoo lo!

I'd hush my boy beside the fountain,
By the soothing, silvery fountain,
On the pleasant, purple mountain,
    In the sultry summer.
        Shoheen sho lo, Shoheen hoo lo!

I would smooth my darling's pillow,
By the blue Atlantic billow,
On the shores of Parknasilla,
    In the golden autumn.
        Shoheen sho lo, Shoheen hoo lo!

I would soothe my child to slumber,
By the rosy, rustling ember,
Through the days of dark December,
    In the stormy winter.
        Shoheen sho lo, Shoheen hoo lo!

May no cruel fairy charm thee!
May no dread banshee alarm thee!
Flood, nor fire, nor sickness harm thee!
    Winter, spring, and summer,—
    Summer, autumn, winter,
        Shoheen sho lo, Shoheen hoo lo!

THE FOGGY DEW.

Oh! a wan cloud was drawn
O'er the dim, weeping dawn,
As to Shannon's side I returned at last;
And the heart in my breast
For the girl I loved best
Was beating—ah beating, how loud and fast!
While the doubts and the fears
Of the long, aching years
Seemed mingling their voices with the moaning flood;
Till full in my path,
Like a wild water-wraith,
My true love's shadow lamenting stood.

But the sudden sun kissed
The cold, cruel mist
Into dancing showers of diamond dew;
The dark flowing stream
Laughed back to his beam,
And the lark soared singing aloft in the blue;
While no phantom of night,
But a form of delight
Ran with arms outspread to her darling boy:
And the girl I love best
On my wild, throbbing breast
Hid her thousand treasures, with a cry of joy.

THE CONFESSION.

A lovely lass with modest mien
  Stole out one morning early;
The dew-drops glancing o'er the green
  Made all her pathway pearly.
Young Lawrence struck with Cupid's dart,—
  Cupid's dart distressing,—
As through the fields he saw her start,
  Sighed, "She's gone confessing!
O vo! 'twould ease *my* heart
  To earn the father's blessing."

The Father, with a twinkling eye,
  He watched my boyo cunning,
Unnoticed by his colleen's eye
  Behind the bushes running.
"How well," he laughed, "young Lawrence there,
  After all my pressing,
With his sweetheart, I declare,
  Comes at last confessing.
Oho! I'll just take care
  To give the lad a lesson."

The pleasant priest unbarred the door,
    As solemn as a shadow,
"How slow," cried he, "you've come before,
    How hot-foot now, my laddo.
The serious steal with looks sedate,
    Seeking to be shriven,
But you, you're in no fitting state
    Now to be forgiven,
So go within and wait
    With all your thoughts on heaven."

The fair one following in a while
    Made out her faults with meekness;
The priest then asked her with a smile
    Had she no other weakness,
And led with that young Lawrence in;
    Her cheeks were now confessing.
"Well, since 'tis after all a sin
    Easy of redressing,
Here, dear, I'd best begin
    To give you both my blessing."

MAUREEN, MAUREEN!

Oh! Maureen, Maureen, have you forgotten
    The fond confession that you made to me,
While round us fluttered the white bog cotton,
    And o'er us waved the wild arbutus tree?
Like bits of sky bo-peeping through the bower,
    No sooner were your blue eyes sought than flown,
Till white and fluttering as the cotton flower
    Your slender hand it slipped into my own.

Oh! Maureen, Maureen, do you remember
    The faithful promise that you pledged to me
The night we parted in black December
    Beneath the tempest-tossed arbutus tree,
When faster than the drops from heaven flowing
    Your heavy tears they showered with ceaseless start,
And wilder than the storm-wind round us blowing
    Your bitter sobs they smote upon my heart?

Oh! Maureen, Maureen, for your love only
  I left my father and mother dear;
Within the churchyard they're lying lonely,
  'Tis from their tombstone I've travelled here.
Their only son, you sent me o'er the billow,
  Ochone! though kneeling they implored me stay;
They sickened with no child to smooth their pillow;
  They died.   Are you as dead to me as they?

Oh! Maureen, must then the love I bore you—
  Seven lonesome summers of longing trust—
Turn like the fortune I've gathered for you,
  Like treacherous fairy treasure, into dust?
But Maureen bawn asthore, your proud lips quiver;
  Into your scornful eyes the tears they start;
Your rebel hand returns to mine for ever;
  Oh! Maureen, Maureen, never more we'll part.

WHEN I ROSE IN THE MORNING.

When I rose in the morning,
    My heart full of woe,
I implored all the song birds
    Why their mates on the bough
To their pleading gave heeding,
    While Kate still said "No;"
But they made no kind answer
    To a heart full of woe.

Till the wood-quest at noon,
    From the forest below,
He taught me his secret
    So tender and low
Of stealing fond feeling
    With sweet notes of woe,
Coo-cooing so soft
    Through the green leafy row.

The long shadows fell,
    And the sun he sank low,
And again I was pleading
    In the mild evening glow:
"Ah! Kitty, have pity!"
    Then how could she say "No."
So for ever I'm free
    From a heart full of woe.

'TIS A PITY I CAN'T SEE MY LOVE.

On his flute of gold the blackbird bold
Love's tale to his melting mate has told,
  And now the thieves have started;
And o'er the ground, in fluttering round,
Enamoured fly, whilst you and I
  In lonesome pain are parted.
But when hearts beat true through the night of sorrow,
They're blest the more when the magic morrow
  Its rosy ray has darted.
  Fortune may wave her wings and fly,
  But she'll flutter back again by and by,
  And crown the constant-hearted.

These birds that pair in the April air
Forget their faith on the branches bare,
  By autumn blasts affrighted,
And to fresh loves sing with the start of spring;
When you and I with a golden ring
  In joy shall be united.
For when hearts beat true through the night of sorrow,
They're blest the most when the marriage morrow
  Its lamp of love has lighted.
  Fortune may wave her wings and fly,
  But she'll flutter back to us by and by,
  And crown the troth we've plighted.

WITH THE NORTH.

With lip contemptuous curling,
   She cried, "Is our flag above
Fold on fold unfurling,
   And Patrick pleading love?
Oh! yes, when patriots hand in hand
Unite to free their foster-land
From slavery's accursed band,
   What true man woos a woman?
Then with my bitter scorning
   Go, live and die a slave,
Or in the morning
   March out with the brave."

"We'll steal a march on sorrow,"
   He sighed, our Captain grey,
"Sound the drum to-morrow
   Before the dawn of day."
But ere the drum's first muffled beat
The women crowded down the street,
How many never more to meet
   Their death-devoted heroes.
Thus as we left the city
   My proud one weeping came
Full of sweet pity,
   And blessed, and blessed my name.

Oh! have you seen Atlantic
   Advance his green, resistless line
Against the cliffs gigantic,
   And bury them in brine?
Thus on our stubborn foe we fell,
Death's lightning darting from our steel,
Whilst round us every cannon peal
   A hero's requiem thundered!
And still with forward faces
   Went down our dauntless men,
And still to their places
   As gallant hearts stepped in.

Till to a sunburst glorious,
   That all the field of battle fired,
Before our van victorious
   The sullen South retired.
Then peace returned, and from the war
Our banner bright with many a star
'Twas mine to flutter from afar
   In triumph to our city;
Till I at last could wreathe it
   Around my true love's heart,
And we kissed beneath it,
   Oh! never more to part.

JENNY, I'M NOT JESTING.

"Ah, Jenny, I'm not jesting,
  Believe what I'm protesting,
  And yield what I'm requesting
    These seven years through."
"Ah, Lawrence, I may grieve you;
  Yet, if I can't relieve you,
  Sure, why should I deceive you
    With words untrue.
But, since you must be courtin',
There's Rosy and her fortune,
'Tis rumoured your consortin'
    With her of late.
Or there's your cousin Kitty,
So charming and so witty,
She'd wed you out of pity,
    Kind Kate."

"Fie! Jenny, since I knew you,
  Of all the lads that woo you,
  None's been so faithful to you,
    If truth were told;
Even when yourself was dartin'
Fond looks at fickle Martin,
Till off the thief went startin'
    For Sheela's gold."
"And, if you've known me longest,
  Why should your love be strongest,
  And his that's now the youngest,
    For that be worst?"
"Fire, Jenny, quickest kindled
Is always soonest dwindled,
And thread the swiftest spindled
    Snaps first."

"If that's your wisdom, Larry,
  The longer I can tarry,
  The luckier I shall marry
    At long, long last."
"I've known of girls amusing,
  Their minds, the men refusing,
  Till none were left for choosing
    At long, long last."

"Well, since it seems that marriage
  Is still the safest carriage,
  And all the world disparage
    The spinster lone;
Since you might still forsake me,
I think I'll let you take me.
Yes! Larry, you may make me
    Your own!"

THE HOUR WE PARTED.

The hour we parted,
When broken-hearted
You clung around me,
  Maureen, aroo,
I swore I'd treasure,
Thro' pain and pleasure,
Thro' health and sickness,
  My love for you.
And still that jewel,
Thro' changes cruel
Of fickle Fortune
  I'll jealous guard;
Still let her vary,
The jade contràry,
If but my Mary
  Be my reward.

Yes! scorn and anger,
Distress and languor,
They're welcome willing,
  The long day thro',
Could I feel certain
That ev'ning's curtain
But clos'd us nearer,
  Maureen, aroo!

The dreamy shadows
Along the meadows
Go softly stealing,
  And falls the dew;
And o'er the billows,
Like faithful swallows,
All, all my thoughts, dear,
  Fly home to you.

With touches silken,
I see you milking
The crossest Kerry
  In Adragole;
And like a fairy
You're singing, Mary,
Till every keeler
  Is foaming full.
The night is falling,
And you are calling
The cattle homeward,
  With coaxing tone;
In God's own keeping,
Awake or sleeping,
'Tis now I leave you,
  Maureen, mavrone!

THE SMITH'S SONG.

"Ding dong, didilium! the big sledge is swinging,
Ding dong, didilium! the little hammer's ringing,
Ding dong, didilium! set the bellows snoring:
Ding dong, didilium! the red fire is roaring.
Hush, boys, and hark, boys, I hear a pair eloping,
Hush, boys, and hark, boys, they'll go free, I'm hoping,
Ding dong, didilium! I hear a shoe clinking,
Ding dong, didilium! there's need of nails, I'm thinking.
*Ding dong, didilium! the big sledge is swinging,
Ding dong, didilium! the little hammer's ringing.*"

"For Heaven's sake, a shoe, smith!" "Your honor, here 'tis ready;
Woa, mare, and so, mare, and steady, girl, steady!
Ding dong, didilium! off goes the carriage,
Ding dong, didilium! good luck be with the marriage.—*Ding dong, &c.*

"Hush, boys, and hark, boys, I hear the kettle drumming,
'Drimin dhu, drimin dhu,' King James's horse are coming;
Up, on the thatch, where my pretty pikes are hidden,
And have them all handy and bright when you're bidden."—*Ding dong, &c.*

"For Heaven's sake, the pikes, smith!" "They're here for your picking,
Long pikes and strong pikes, and pikes for Dutchmen-sticking!
Ding dong, didilium! cursing in their cruppers,
Here jog the Mynherrs, 'tis time for our suppers."—*Ding dong, &c.*

PLERACA.

Beimeedh a gole!
Fill up the bowl,
Let us console
Dull care with a glass, boys!
Shall it be wine,
Fragrant and fine,
Fresh smuggled from Spain underneath a mattràss, boys?
No! all of those pleasant
Casks out of Cadiz
Leave as a present,
Lads, for the ladies!
But for ourselves, sure
What should we say
But Whiskey for ever!
Till dawning of day.

MUSIC.

Beimeedh a gole!
Wasn't it droll,
He that first stole
Fire from Heaven's grate, boys,
Look now, was left,
Chained to a cleft,
A century through, for an aigle to ate, boys!
St. Pat, though, when stealing
Fire from that quarter,
Kept it concealing
Snug under water;
Till he'd conveyed it
Safe to the ground,
Then looked, and, begorra,
'Twas *whiskey* he found.

Beimeedh a gole!
Each with his poll
Quite in control,
For all its containing;
Smiling we sit,
Warming our wit
With nectar the Gods might begrudge us the draining.
Now, ere we go snoozing
Under the clothes,
Don't be refusing
One health I propose.
Here's to the darling,
Pale as the dew,
That pounds Purple Bacchus
And all of his crew!

SONG OF THE GHOST.

When all were dreaming
  But Pastheen Power,
A light came streaming
  Beneath her bower:
A heavy foot
  At her door delayed,
A heavy hand
  On the latch was laid.

"Now who dare venture,
  At this dark hour,
Unbid to enter
  My maiden bower?"
"Dear Pastheen, open
  The door to me,
And your true lover
  You'll surely see."

"My own true lover,
  So tall and brave,
Lives exiled over
  The angry wave."
"Your true love's body
  Lies on the bier,
His faithful spirit
  Is with you here."

"His look was cheerful,
  His voice was gay;
Your speech is fearful,
  Your face is grey;
And sad and sunken
  Your eye of blue,
But Patrick, Patrick,
  Alas! 'tis you!"

Ere dawn was breaking
  She heard below
The two cocks shaking
  Their wings to crow.
"Oh, hush you, hush you,
  Both red and grey,
Or you will hurry
  My love away.

"Oh, hush your crowing,
  Both grey and red,
Or he'll be going
  To join the dead;
Oh, cease from calling
  His ghost to the mould,
And I'll come crowning
  Your combs with gold."

When all were dreaming
  But Pastheen Power,
A light went streaming
  From out her bower;
And on the morrow,
  When they awoke,
They knew that sorrow
  Her heart had broke.

COLLEEN OGE ASTHORE.

When I marched away to war,
How you kissed me o'er and o'er:
    Weeping, pressed me;
    Sobbing, blessed me;
Colleen, colleen oge asthore.

I was wounded, wounded sore,
Dead, your father falsely swore;
    Mad to harry
    You to marry
One with miser-gold in store.

Ah! but when you dreamed me dead,
Forth you flew a wildered maid:
    Ever grieving,
    Ever weaving
Willow, willow for your head.

"Nay, he lives," your mother said,
But you only shook your head;
    "Why deceive me?
    Ah! believe me,
Mother, mother, he is dead."

So you pined and pined away,
Till, when in the winter grey
    Home I hasted,
    Wan and wasted,
Colleen, colleen oge, you lay.

"'Tis his lonesome ghost," you said,
"Come to call me to the dead;"
    "Nay, discover
    Your dear lover
Longing now at last to wed."

Then your cheek, so pale before,
With the rose of hope once more,
    Faintly, slowly,
    Brightly, wholly,
Blossomed, colleen oge asthore.

Till upon the chapel floor,
Side by side, we knelt and swore,
    Duty dearest,
    Love sincerest,
Colleen, colleen oge asthore.

THE FLIGHT OF THE EARLS.

To other shores across the sea
  We speed with swelling sail;
Yet still there lingers on our lee
  A phantom Innisfail.
Oh fear, fear not, gentle ghost,
  Your sons shall turn untrue!
Though fain to fly your lovely coast,
  They leave their hearts with you.

As slowly into distance dim
  Your shadow sinks and dies,
So o'er the ocean's utmost rim
  Another realm shall rise;
New hills shall swell, new vales expand,
  New rivers winding flow,
But could we for a foster land
  Your mother-love forego?

Shall mighty Espan's martial praise
  Our patriot pulses still,
And o'er your memory's fervent rays
  For ever cast a chill?
Oh, no! we live for your relief,
  Till home from alien earth
We share the smile that gilds your grief,
  The tear that gems your mirth.

A SAILOR LOVED A FARMER'S DAUGHTER.

A sailor once wooed a farmer's daughter,
　The fairest lass in all the country side.
She loved him well; but when he besought her
　With beating, beating heart to be his bride,
"A sailor lad," she said, "I'll never, never wed,
　And live a wife and widow all in one;
O no, my charmer shall be a farmer,
　Returning faithful with the set of sun."

At danger's call, across the water
   The sailor went, but left his heart behind;
Fresh lovers whispered the farmer's daughter;
   Yet when they prayed her to confess her mind,
"A farmer's lad," she said, "I'll never, never wed,
   When heroes bleed to guard their native strand.
Till war is over I need no lover:
   Then let the stoutest soldier claim my hand."

When peace returned, escaped from slaughter,
   With stars and crosses home our warriors came,
And some went wooing the farmer's daughter,
   But none could charm the lass to change her name;
Until once more from far a gallant, gallant tar
   Began with beating heart his love to tell;
And sweetly turning, with blushes burning,
   She sighed: "Since first we met I've loved you well!"

FATHER O'FLYNN.

Of priests we can offer a charmin' variety,
Far renowned for larnin' and piety ;
Still, I'd advance ye widout impropriety,
   Father O'Flynn as the flower of them all.

Chorus.

Here's a health to you, Father O'Flynn,
Slainté, and slainté, and slainté agin ;
   Powerfulest preacher, and
   Tinderest teacher, and
Kindliest creature in ould Donegal.

Don't talk of your Provost and Fellows of Trinity,
Famous for ever at Greek and Latinity,
Faix and the divels and all at Divinity,
   Father O'Flynn 'd make hares of them all !
   Come, I vinture to give ye my word,
   Never the likes of his logic was heard,
     Down from mythology
     Into thayology,
Troth ! and conchology if he'd the call.—*Chorus.*

Och ! Father O'Flynn you've the wonderful way wid you,
All ould sinners are wishful to pray wid you,
All the young childer are wild for to play wid you,
   You've such a way wid you, Father avick !
     Still for all you've so gentle a soul,
      Gad, you've your flock in the grandest control;
       Checking the crazy ones,
       Coaxin' onaisy ones,
Liftin' the lazy ones on wid the stick.—*Chorus.*

And though quite avoidin' all foolish frivolity,
Still at all seasons of innocent jollity,
Where was the play-boy could claim an equality
   At comicality, Father, wid you?
     Once the Bishop looked grave at your jest,
     Till this remark set him off wid the rest:
       " Is it lave gaiety
        All to the laity?
Cannot the clergy be Irishmen too?"—*Chorus.*

'TWAS PRETTY TO BE IN BALLINDERRY.

'Twas pretty to be in Ballinderry,
   'Twas pretty to be in Aghalee,
'Twas prettier to be in little Ram's Island,
   Trysting under the ivy tree!
      Ochone, ochone!
      Ochone, ochone!
For often I roved in little Ram's Island,
Side by side with Phelimy Hyland,
And still he'd court me and I'd be coy,
Though at heart I loved him, my handsome boy!

"I'm going," he sighed, "from Ballinderry
   Out and across the stormy sea;
Then if in your heart you love me, Mary,
   Open your arms at last to me."
      Ochone, ochone!
      Ochone, ochone!
I opened my arms; how well he knew me!
I opened my arms and took him to me;
And there, in the gloom of the groaning mast,
We kissed our first and we kissed our last!

Twas happy to be in little Ram's Island,
  But now 'tis sad as sad can be;
For the ship that sailed with Phelimy Hyland
  Is sunk for ever beneath the sea.
        Ochone, ochone!
        Ochone, ochone!
And 'tis oh! but I wear the weeping willow,
And wander alone by the lonesome billow,
And cry to him over the cruel sea,
  "Phelimy Hyland, come back to me!"

MY BONNY CUCKOO.

My bonny cuckoo, come whisper true!
Around the world I'd rove with you;
I'd rove with you until the next spring,
And still my cuckoo would sweetly sing,—
"Cuckoo! cuckoo!" until the next spring;
"Cuckoo! cuckoo!" until the next spring.

The ash and the hazel shall mourning say,—
"Oh, merry cuckoo, don't fly away!
The winter wind is rude and keen;
Oh, cuckoo, stay and keep us green!
Cuckoo! cuckoo! oh stay! oh stay!
And make the season for ever May!"

The thrush and the robin shall sadly cry,—
"Our bonny cuckoo, oh, do not fly!
For when you spread your speckled wing
We have no longer heart to sing.
Cuckoo, cuckoo, still lead our tune,
And make the season for ever June!"

The lads and the lasses together stand,
And call their cuckoo from off the strand,—
"How can you leave us, bird of love,
With the green below and the blue above?
Oh no! oh no! you shall not go,
With the blue above and the green below."

JACK THE JOLLY PLOUGHBOY.

As Jack the jolly ploughboy was ploughing through his land,
He turned his share and shouted to bid his horses stand,
Then down beside his team he sat, contented as a king,
And Jack he sang his song so sweet he made the mountains ring
        With his Ta-ran-nan nanty na,
        Sing ta-ran-nan nanty na,
    While the mountains all ringing re-echoed the singing
        Of ta-ran-nan nanty na.

'Tis said old England's sailors, when wintry tempests roar,
Will plough the stormy waters, and pray for those on shore;
But through the angry winter the share, the share for me,
To drive a steady furrow, and pray for those at sea.
        With my Ta-ran-nan nanty na, &c., &c.

When heaven above is bluest, and earth most green below,
Away from wife and sweetheart the fisherman must go,
But golden seed I'll scatter beside the girl I love
And smile to hear the cuckoo and sigh to hear the dove,
                With my Ta-ran-nan nanty na, &c., &c.

'Tis oft the hardy fishers a scanty harvest earn
And gallant tars from glory on wooden legs return,
But a bursting crop for ever shall dance before my flail,
For I'll live and die a farmer all in the Golden Vale.
                With my Ta-ran-nan nanty na, &c., &c.

CAOINE.

Cold, dark, and dumb lies my boy on his bed;
Cold, dark, and silent the night dews are shed;
Hot, swift, and fierce fall my tears for the dead!

His footprints lay light in the dew of the dawn
As the straight, slender track of the young mountain fawn;
But I'll ne'er again follow them over the lawn.

His manly cheek blushed with the sun's rising ray,
And he shone in his strength like the sun at midday;
But a cloud of black darkness has hid him away.

And that black cloud for ever shall cling to the skies:
And never, ah, never, I'll see him arise,
Lost warmth of my bosom, lost light of my eyes!

THE REJECTED LOVER.

On Innisfallen's fairy isle,
  Amid the blooming bushes, O!
We leant upon the lover's stile,
  And listened to the thrushes, O!
When first I sighed to see her smile,
  And smiled to see her blushes, O!

Her hair was bright as beaten gold,
  And soft as spider's spinning, O!
Her cheek out-bloomed the apple old
  That set our parents sinning, O!
And in her eyes you might behold
  My joys and griefs beginning, O!

In Innisfallen's fairy grove
  I hushed my happy wooing, O!
To listen to the brooding dove
  Amid the branches cooing, O!
But oh! how short those hours of love,
  How long their bitter rueing, oh!

Poor cushat thy complaining breast
  With woe like mine is heaving, oh!
With thee I mourn a fruitless quest,
  For ah! with art deceiving, oh!
The cuckoo-bird has robbed my nest,
  And left me wildly grieving, oh!

IRISH SPINNING WHEEL SONG.

      Show me a sight
      Bates for delight
An ould Irish wheel wid a young Irish girl at it.
      O! No!
      Nothin' you'll show
Aquals her sittin' and takin' a twirl at it.

      Look at her there,
      Night in her hair—
The blue ray of day from her eye laughin' out on us!
      Faix, an' a foot,
      Perfect of cut,
Peepin' to put an end to all doubt in us

      That there's a sight
      Bates for delight
An ould Irish wheel wid a young Irish girl at it.
      O! No!
      Nothin' you'll show
Aquals her sittin' an' takin' a twirl at it.

      How the lamb's wool
      Turns coarse an' dull
By them soft, beautiful, weeshy, white hands of her;
      Down goes her heel,
      Roun' runs the reel,
Purrin' wid pleasure to take the commands of her.

>   Then show me a sight
>   Bates for delight
> An ould Irish wheel wid a young Irish girl at it.
>   O! No!
>   Nothin' you'll show
> Aquals her sittin' an' takin' a twirl at it.
>
>   Talk of Three Fates,
>   Seated on seats,
> Spinnin' and shearin' away till they've done for me.
>   You may want three
>   For your massacree;
> But one fate for me, boys, and only the one for me.
>
>   And
>   Isn't that fate,
>   Pictured complate,
> An ould Irish wheel wid a young Irish girl at it?
>   O! No!
>   Nothin' you'll show
> Aquals her sittin' an' takin' a twirl at it.

IRISH LULLABY.

I'd rock my own sweet childie to rest in a cradle of gold on a bough of the willow,
To the *shoheen sho* of the wind of the west and the *sho hoo lo* of the soft sea billow.
    Sleep, baby dear,
    Sleep without fear,
  Mother is here beside your pillow.

I'd put my own sweet childie to sleep in a silver boat on the beautiful river,
Where a *shoheen* whisper the white cascades, and a *sho hoo lo* the green flags shiver.
    Sleep, baby dear,
    Sleep without fear,
  Mother is here with you for ever.

Sho hoo lo! to the rise and fall of mother's bosom 'tis sleep has bound you,
And O, my child, what cozier nest for rosier rest could love have found you?
    Sleep, baby dear,
    Sleep without fear,
  Mother's two arms are clasped around you.

GOOD NIGHT.

Now! good night! our feast is ending,
Where in laughing troops attending;
Wit and worth and beauty blending
　　Sped the hours with dance and song.
　　　　Beauty's smile
　　　　Free from guile,
　　　　Wit that shone
　　　　Wounding none:
　　And manly worth and woman true,
　　Good night! and joy go home with you.

Good night! and may your minstrel's numbers
Echoing on amid your slumbers,
Spell-bind every care that cumbers
　　Lover's heart, and mother's breast.
　　　　Beauty, mirth,
　　　　Wit and worth
　　　　Fall to sleep
　　　　Calm and deep,
　　Nor rouse, till rosy morrow call,
　　"Awake, and joy go with you all!"

NOTES.

The Little Red Lark.

(See Musical Appendix, p. 203.)

3. This poem was suggested by the following passage from Miss Brooke's now rare "Reliques of Irish Poetry,"[1] p. 232. "In another song, a lover, tenderly reproaching his mistress, asks her, why she keeps morning so long indoors? and bids her come out, and bring him the day." Its title, "The Little Red Lark," is given in Hoffmann's collection of Irish music[2] as the name of an old melody.

Love's Wishes.

(See Musical Appendix, p. 204.)

5. These words are written to a melody in Petrie's collection of Irish music.[3] The first verse is founded upon a Celtic song, of which the two following stanzas in translation have been furnished me by my friend Dr. Joyce:—

> Would God I were a little apple,
>   Or one of the small daisies,
>   Or a rose in the garden
>   Where thou art accustomed to walk alone;
>
> In hope that thou wouldst pluck from me
>   Some wee little branch,
> Which thou wouldst hold in thy right hand
>   Or in the breast of thy robe.

The second verse is original. My words, arranged as a song by Dr. Hiles to the old air printed in the appendix, are published by Forsyth Brothers, of London and Manchester.

I Once Loved a Boy.

(See Musical Appendix, p. 205.)

6. Suggested by and written to an air of this name in Petrie's collection. The words of the original song are as follows:—

---

[1] George Bonham, Dublin, MDCCLXXXIX.

[2] "Ancient Music of Ireland," from the Petrie collection, arranged for the pianoforte by F. Hoffmann. Dublin: Pigott and Co., 112, Grafton Street. 1877.

[3] "The Petrie Collection of the Ancient Music of Ireland," vol. 1. Dublin: Printed at the University Press, for the Society for the Preservation and Publication of the Melodies of Ireland. By M. H. Gill. 1855.

> I once lov'd a boy, and a bonny, bonny boy,
>   Who'd come and go at my request;
> I lov'd him so well, and so very very well,
>   That I built him a bower in my breast—
>   In my breast,
>   That I built him a bower in my breast.
>
> I once lov'd a boy, and a bonny, bonny boy,
>   And a boy that I thought was my own;
> But he loves another girl better than me,
>   And has taken his flight and is gone—
>   And is gone,
>   And has taken his flight and is gone.
>
> The girl that has taken my own bonny boy,
>   Let her make of him all that she can,
> For whether he loves me or he loves me not,
>   I'll walk with my love now and then—
>   Now and then,
>   I'll walk with my love now and then.

6. *Wirrasthrue* = "O Mary and sorrow!"

The Banks of the Daisies.

7. Suggested by a song of this name, but not written directly to the music of it.

Forenint = before, in front of.

Herring is King.

9. Suggested by a song of this name in Horncastle's "Irish Entertainment," which opens in the same way and has the same Irish refrain, the second line of which translates the first. Otherwise the poem is original.

Shawn, Irish for "John."

10. *Góleen* = creek.

Hush Song.

(*See* MUSICAL APPENDIX, p. 206.)

12. Written to an old Irish lullaby in Petrie's collection. The last stanza alone is suggested by a verse in the Celtic original, of which the following is a literal translation:—

> Sleep, my child, and be it the sleep of safety,
> And out of your sleep may you rise in health;
> May neither cholic nor death-stitch strike you,
> The infant's disease, or the ugly small-pox.

PAGE
12. *Laddo*, a playful form of the word "lad." Cf. *boyo*.
    The refrain has no more precise meaning than "Hush-a-bye."
13. *Banshee*. Literally "a woman from the fairy-hills": a sad spirit who is often heard wailing at night, when a member of the family is about to die.

The Foggy Dew.

(*See* Musical Appendix, p. 207.)

14. Suggested by and written to an air of this name in Bunting's collection.[1] There are rustic words to it, but they are not of any literary value. My own words were written before I met with them.

The Confession.

(*See* Musical Appendix, p. 208.)

16. Written to an air in Bunting's collection of Irish music beginning with the words—

    > A lovely lass to a friar came
    > To confess one morning early.

    and suggested by them. I have not been able to procure the rest of the old ballad.
    O vo! an Irish exclamation expressive of sorrow or surprise.
17. *Hot-foot*, a good old English expression implying great haste, commonly used in Munster.

The Girl I left behind me.

18. There are several well-known versions of this song. I need hardly say, therefore, that my words are original except so far as the situation of the singer and the refrain are concerned.
    The *route*, pronounced "rout" by the soldiers = marching orders.

Eva Tuohill.

20. Music has been written to this song by Charles Salaman, and is published by Novello, Ewer, and Co., 1, Berners Street, London, W.

---

[1] "The Ancient Music of Ireland," arranged for the pianoforte by Edward Bunting. Dublin: Hodges and Smith. 1840.

'Tis I can weave Woollen and Linen.

PAGE
22. Written to and suggested by an air, "'Tis I can weave linen and woollen" in Bunting's collection. I have not come across any other words belonging to the original ballad.

Maureen, Maureen.
(*See* MUSICAL APPENDIX, p. 210.)

23. Suggested by the two lines—

> Oh, Nancy, Nancy, don't you remember
> The protestations that you made to me?

which appear in Petrie's collection in connection with the air to which I have written my words.

Arbutus, pronounced "arbútus" in the south of Ireland.

24. *Maureen bawn asthore* = fair-haired little Mary, my treasure.

When I rose in the Morning.
(*See* MUSICAL APPENDIX, p. 212.)

25. Suggested by and written to an air with this title in Petrie's collection.

Wood-quest = wood-pigeon.

The Mill Song.

27. Suggested by a shorter song, the refrain of which I alone make use of, in Horncastle's "Irish Entertainment."

'Tis a pity I can't see my love.
(*See* MUSICAL APPENDIX, p. 213.)

30. Suggested by and written to an air with this title in Bunting's collection. I have not come across any other words belonging to the original ballad.

With the North.
(*See* MUSICAL APPENDIX, p. 214.)

32. An Irish-American ballad written to the air of the "Irish hautboy" (Petrie's collection), but entirely original.

Nancy, the Pride of the West.

35. Suggested by the title of a song, "Nancy, the Pride of the East," but not written to the air that goes by that name.
36. *Tussocks* = tufts.
    For all that = Notwithstanding that.

Jenny, I'm not Jesting.
(See MUSICAL APPENDIX, p. 216.)

37. Written to the air "Biddy, I'm not jesting," in Hoffmann's collection, the title of which is all that I know of the words of the song.

The Hour we Parted.
(See MUSICAL APPENDIX, p. 218.)

40. Written to the air "I'd make my love a breast of glass" in Petrie's and Hoffmann's collections of Irish music.
    Aroo closely corresponds with the exclamations "O dear!" "O dear me!"
41. *Distress* = bodily suffering in Irish peasant parlance.
    Kerry = Kerry cow.
42. *Keeler* = wooden milking vessel.

The Smith's Song.
(See MUSICAL APPENDIX, p. 219.)

43. Written to an air of which Dr. Petrie thus speaks:—"'The Smith's Song' has very evidently been suggested, like Handel's 'Harmonious Blacksmith,' by the measured time and varied tones of his hammers striking upon the anvil."—"Ancient Music of Ireland," p. 171. He also thus quotes from a communication made to him on the subject of the same song by Professor O'Curry: "The song and tune of 'Ding dong, didilium! *Buail seo, seid seo*,' must be one of great antiquity. I scarcely ever heard it sung but to pacify a crying or *cross* infant; and then the woman sang it with a slow swinging motion of her body backwards and forwards, and to either side, with the child in her arms, with no intention, however, to put it to sleep. Sometimes there was no swing of the body; but then the foot went down on the heel and toe alternately, but in such a measure of time as resembled, in some way, the striking of the iron on the smith's

anvil, where he himself gave two blows with his *lamh-ord*, or hand-hammer," the "little hammer" in my song, "for every one blow that the sledger gave with his *ord mor*," my "big sledge,' or sledge hammer.

43.   "*I hear the kettle-drumming,*
         '*Drimin dhu, drimin dhu.*'"

A reference to another old air, used as a party tune during the war (1688–90), "The White-backed Black-haired Cow," representing, by a very strange metaphor, the cause of James II. (See Bunting's collection.)

My words are original, except in so far as they reflect a similar reference to an elopement in T. Irwin's ballad "The Mountain Forge," and are indebted to the refrain of the Celtic song, thus translated by Professor O'Curry:—

        Ding dong, didilium !
        Strike this, blow this;

with regard to which he has written: "It may be objected that the words 'ding dong,' in the burden of this song, are modern; but such is not the fact, for where the 'Annals of the Four Masters' record, at the year 1015, the death of MacLiag, poet and secretary to Brian Boru, they also record the following verse, which it would appear was the last verse the poet composed while on his death-bed, and which contains the very words in question:—

        O bell, which art my pillow's head,
         To visit thee no friends come ;
        Though thou makest thy 'ding dang,'
         It is by thee the salt is measured."

Mo Muirnin Dhu.

45. This title, which signifies "my black-haired darling," was suggested by and written to an air in Petrie's collection, "Mo muirnin oge."

46. *Collogue* = colloquium, chat.

Pleraca.

(*See* MUSICAL APPENDIX, p. 229.)

47. The above term is thus explained by Professor O'Curry: "Wherever the word *Pleraca* occurs in any Irish song or rhyme of the last

NOTES.

hundred years, it is in the sense of an abandonment to drinking, dancing, singing, or love-making, carried out in all imaginable riotous and reckless gaiety, and was, no doubt, looked upon as the ball of the times then passing."—Petrie's "Ancient Music of Ireland," p. 16.

47. *Beimeedh a gole!* = "Let us be drinking," the first words of a Cork drinking song, the music of which, noted from the whistling of an Irish friend, will be found in the musical appendix. My words are written to this air: but borrow only the first line of each stanza from the Irish song.

Mattràss = mattress.

48.
*He that first stole
Fire from Heaven's grate, boys* = Prometheus.

Song of the Ghost.
(*See* MUSICAL APPENDIX, p. 222.)

50. Written to an air in Hoffmann's collection bearing this name.

*And I'll come crowning
Your combs with gold.*

Suggested by this exquisite fragment supplied me by Dr. Joyce, which occurs in a ballad descriptive of the visit of a lover's ghost to his betrothed. Before daybreak, in order to keep him still longer with her, she says:—

"O my pretty cock, O my handsome cock,
 I pray you do not crow before day,
And your comb shall be made of the very beaten gold,
 And your wings of the silver so gray."

Colleen Oge Asthore.

53. Air, "Callino Casturame," Hoffmann's collection.

NOTE.—"It is evidently to this tune that Shakespeare alludes in the play of Henry V., act iv., scene 4, where Pistol, on meeting a French soldier, exclaims, 'Quality! Calen, O custure me.' In the folio we find 'Calmie custure me,' which has been turned in the modern editions into 'Call you me? Construe me.' Malone found among 'Sundry new Sonets in a handefull of pleasant Delites 1584' a sonnet of a lover in praise of his lady to 'Calen, O custure me,' sung at every line's end. In Mr.

Lover's 'Lyrics of Ireland,' he notices the resemblance of the first word to the name 'Caillino,' speaking of Mrs. Fitzsimon's beautiful poem, 'The Woods of Caillino,' and adds: 'Mr. Boswell, in his edition of Shakespeare, says that Mr. Finnegan, master of the school established in London for the education of the Irish, says the words mean "Little girl of my heart for ever and ever."' Now this is not the meaning, and I cannot but wonder that, with so much literary discussion as has taken place on the subject, the true spelling and consequently the meaning of the burden have remained till now undiscovered. The burden, as given in the 'Handefull of pleasant Delites,' and copied by Malone, is 'Calen O custure me,' which is an attempt to spell and pretty nearly represents the sound of 'Colleen oge astore,' and these words mean 'Young girl, my treasure.'"—Stokes' "Life of Petrie," p. 431, quoted by Hoffmann in his "Ancient Music of Ireland," p. 137.

This interesting air is taken from Queen Elizabeth's Virginal Book, and is published by Mr. W. Chappell in his "English Music of the Olden Time." I have the permission of Messrs. Chappell to reproduce it in my musical appendix, where it will be found at p. 223.

The Flight of the Earls.
(*See* MUSICAL APPENDIX, p. 224.)

56. "Tyrone deliberately gave up the national cause, when resistance was no longer possible; and, submitting to the inevitable, proposed to hold his earldom as an English subject." . . . "If he had fallen sword in hand, the English might have felt the sympathy due to a gallant foe; but that six years of warfare, costly and bloody, should have left Hugh O'Neill the Earl of Tyrone, was a very unsatisfactory result." . . . "Day by day he must have learned, by a continuous course of litigation and insult, that he was a marked man." . . . "Exactly in the same position as the earl was Rory O'Donnell, who, following the example of Tyrone, had submitted to, and received from, the English Government the title of Earl of Tyrconnell. For some years the two earls led a most uncomfortable and not a very dignified life, until, in 1607, when O'Neill proposed to try his grievances before James I. in London. Hearing, however, that

he would there be arrested on a charge of conspiracy, he availed himself of the despatch by his friend Cuconaught Maguire of an armed ship from Flanders to the north of Ireland to assist his departure. The Earl of Tyrconnell resolved to accompany him; they both fled with their families, and succeeded in embarking in Maguire's vessel in the Lough Swilly."—Richey's "Lectures on Irish History: Second Series," E. Ponsonby, 116, Grafton Street, Dublin.

56. *Innisfail*, an ancient poetical name of Ireland.
57. *Espan* = Spain.

Kitty Bhan.

58. Suggested by and written to an Irish ballad and air, "O Woman of the House," in Petrie's collection; indeed, an adaptation of the original Celtic, thus translated by the late Edward Walsh:[1]

> Before the sun rose at yester-dawn,
> I met a fair maid adown the lawn;
> The berry and snow to her cheek gave its glow,
> And her bosom was fair as the sailing swan.
> Then, pulse of my heart! what gloom is thine?
>
> Her beautiful voice more hearts hath won
> Than Orpheus' lyre of old had done;
> Her ripe eyes of blue were crystals of dew,
> On the grass of the lawn before the sun.
> And, pulse of my heart! what gloom is thine?

Kitty Bhan or *Bawn* = Fair-haired Kitty.

The White Blossom's off the Bog.

59. Suggested by the first line of the following couplet, translated from the Celtic on p. 8 of Petrie's collection:—

> "The white blossom is on the bogs and autumn is on the return,
> And though marriage is a pretty, pretty thing, 'tis sorrowful and tearful it has left me."

With Fluttering Joy.

60. The first of these two stanzas is founded upon the following verse, translated thus by Dr. Joyce from the Irish:—

---

[1] "Irish Popular Songs, with English Metrical Translations," by the late Edward Walsh. Dublin: James M'Glashan. 1847.

> How delightful for the little birds
> Who rise up on high,
> Who are accustomed to warble with each other
> On the same branch.
>
> Not so is it with me and
> My hundred thousand loves;
> It is far from each other
> Each day finds us when it dawns.

The second stanza is original.

A Sailor loved a Farmer's Daughter.

(*See* Musical Appendix, p. 225.)

61. Suggested by and written to an air in Bunting's collection. The following four lines, for which I am indebted to Dr. Joyce, will give an idea of the character of the popular ballad to this fine tune:—

> A sailor courted a farmer's daughter
> Who lived convenient to the Isle of Man.
> Remark, good people, what followed after,—
> A long time courting and nothing done.

The Reaper's Revenge.

63. Suggested by and written to the air of "Beside the White Rock," but founded upon no earlier words to that melody.
Acora = my friend.

The Blue, Blue Smoke.

65. This song was suggested in part by a letter written me by my friend Dr. Joyce, in which the words "the dim old days" occurred; in part by a song by his brother, Dr. R. D. Joyce, entitled the "Yellow, Yellow Hair."
The chapel's distant chime = The angelus bell.
Coom = valley.

66. *Herself* = the wife. Himself and herself are thus used in the south of Ireland to imply the master and mistress of the house.

Father O'Flynn.

(*See* MUSICAL APPENDIX, p. 227.)

PAGE
71. *Slainté* = your health.
    Trinity = Dublin University.
72. *Make hares of them* = utterly rout and put to flight in argument, a common Irish peasant phrase.
    Avick = my son; a palpable bull in the context.

Molleen Oge.

74. The title means "Young little Molly."
    Brogue = shoe.
75. *The vogue* = the fashion.

Two Irish Idylls.

76. *Yerrig!* an exclamation addressed to the pony = our "Jick!" or "gee-up!"
77. *Pogue* = kiss.

Fan Fitzgerl.

79. *Fitzgerl*, a slovenly pronunciation of "Fitzgerald."
    Wirra, wirra! ologone! exclamations of distress.
    Cot = caught.
80. *Apast* = past.
    Beyant = beyond.

Bat of the Bridge.

81. *Bat* or *Batsy*, the short for "Bartholomew."
82. *Thrun away* = thrown away.
    Proper man = fine, hearty man.
    A broth of a boy = a choice spirit.
    Adragole, pronounced as though written "Adragool."
83. *Unknownst* = unnoticed.
85. *Iday* = idea.
    Fellas = fellows.
    Bellas = bellows.
    Give them a twist = hurt, injure.
    Corney = Cornelius.
    Bad scran = bad luck.

The Light in the Snow.

PAGE
87. *Sorra letter* = not one letter, alas!
Kep = kept.
88. *The overside* = the opposite side.
Callin' you in church. Relatives and friends of Irish emigrants in the States whom they have lost sight of are assisted in getting tidings of them by the American priests, who, during service in church, ask their congregations for information about them.
Mavrone = my sorrow! alas!
89. *Windy* = window.

What is Life widout a Wife?

90. *Festal Chorus.* This poem partakes of the nature of the "Loobeen," for an explanation of which see page 255.

The Wreck of the Aideen.

93. *God incrase ye* = God prosper you.
Mortial = mortal.
Distress me = hurt me.
94. *Ologone!* an exclamation of deep sorrow.
Machree = my heart.
Agra, a term of endearment; dear love.

The Handsome Witch.

96. *Many a colleen in the dairy, &c.* The waving of the churnstaff and the scattering of salt were and, indeed, are counter-charms employed to baffle the pranks supposed to be played by witches and fairies upon Irish dairies.
97. *Thry for butter;* i.e., lift the lid or save-all of the churn, and test the milk for butter with a spoon.
Morna drew the dead-man's hand. "When no butter would come the witch was at that moment in her cavern, seated on her heels before a vessel of water, from which, by drawing a deadman's hand through it, she appropriated the produce of other people's honest labour." Thus write the brothers Banim in their tale of "The Hare-hound and the Witch."

Sabing the Turf.

PAGE
98. *Slan* (the *a* sounded long as in " far ") = the narrow spade used for *cutting* or digging up the *turf* or peat.

The bawn = home-field for cattle.

Footin' = laying out the sods of turf lengthways. *Settin'* = setting up two or three of the peats endways against one another.

The say-turn = the sea-breeze which commonly sets in on a fine summer's afternoon.

Drawin' = carting away the peat.

The boats are out in the bay; *i.e.*, for fishing purposes.

Haggard = hay-yard.

Loobeen.

99. "The Loobeen," writes Mr. Bunting, quoted by Dr. Petrie in his "Ancient Music of Ireland," "is a peculiar species of chant, having a well-marked time, and a frequently recurring chorus or catch-word. It is sung at merry-makings and assemblages of the young women, when they meet at 'spinnings' and 'quiltings,' and is accompanied by extemporaneous verses of which each singer successively furnishes a line. The intervention of the chorus after each line gives time for the preparation of the succeeding one by the next singer, and thus the Loobeen goes round until the chain of song is completed."

After comparing the Loobeen to the Highland Luinniochs, Dr. Petrie thus quotes Professor O'Curry: "Sometimes the group consisted of the daughters of the house, and neighbouring poorer girls, who are engaged for hire at—say in 1816—threepence a day each. Sometimes it was the *comhar* or reciprocal cooperation of the daughters of two or more neighbouring families; but, in all cases, the work—particularly wool-spinning—was carried on with an accompaniment of singing. . . . Generally they sang, two at a time, extemporaneous verses to peculiar airs, to none of which have I ever heard songs or verses of another kind."

A specimen of the **Loobeen** is then added, every line of which is preceded and followed by the **crambe** words *Mallo lero, and eembo nero,—Mallo lero, and eembo* **bawn,** as follows :—

"I traversed the wood when day was breaking."
"For John O'Carroll you wandered so early."

"With gads begirt, let him plough through Erinn!"
"You mannerless girl, he is your match for a husband."
"I care not, leave off, get me my own love!"
"Thomas O'Maddigan, take and be pleased with."
"I take, and hail, and may I well wear my husband."
"To the east or the west may you never be parted."
"Go westward, go eastward, and find me my own love."
"Donnell O'Flaherty, take and be pleased with."
"It's Joan O'Kelly that would strike me in the face."
"If the man is worth it, don't let her take him."
"There's no tree in the wood that I could not find its equal."

My poem is founded on this translation from a Celtic original, but is irregular as a Loobeen in that it dispenses with a refrain. Neither is it written to a Loobeen air.

99. *With your pippen, &c.* Preference on the part of a girl for a young man amongst the Cork and Kerry peasantry was, if it is not still, shown by throwing an apple at the object of affection. Readers of Virgil will of course at once think of *Malo me Galatea petit.*

100. *Murt-na-mo* = Murtogh of the cows, or with the good herd of cattle.

101. *The model teacher* = a teacher in one of the Government Model Schools.

The Black '46.

102. *A sacred tree.* One of the old trees which are still objects of reverence in different parts of Ireland, owing to their actual or supposed connection with some early saint, or on some such other religious ground.

Two boreens = two little roads; two deep lanes.

103. *Yous* = you.
Crep = crept.
Unbeknownst = unnoticed.
Spuds = potatoes.

104. *Folly* = follow.

Shuile Agra.

107. My version of this ballad is founded upon the two following editions of it, which are printed side by side for comparison with each other and with my own. The first of them was obtained by me from the Library of the Royal Irish Academy;

the second is copied from a broadsheet picked up by my friend
Dr. Joyce :—

SHUILE AGRA.

As I roved through my new garden bowers,
To gaze upon fast fading flowers,
And think upon the happiest hours
    That fled in Summer's bloom.
  Shuile, shuile, shuile agra,
  Time can only ease my woe;
  Since the lad of my heart from me did go,
    Gotheen mavourneen slaun.

'Tis often I sat on my true love's knee,
And many a fond story he told me;
He told me things that ne'er would be,
    Gotheen mavourneen slaun.
      Shuile, shuile, &c.

I'll sell my rock, I'll sell my reel,
When flax is spun I'll sell my wheel,
To buy my love a sword and shield,
    Gotheen mavourneen slaun.
      Shuile, shuile, &c.

I'll dye my petticoat, I'll dye it red,
And round the world I'll beg my bread,
That all my friends would wish me dead,
    Gotheen mavourneen slaun.
      Shuile, shuile, &c.

I wish I was on Brandon Hill,
'Tis there I'll sit and cry my fill,
That every tear would turn a mill,
    Gotheen mavourneen slaun.
      Shuile, shuile, &c.

No more am I that blooming maid,
That used to rove the valley shade,
My youth and bloom are all decayed,
    Gotheen mavourneen slaun.
      Shuile, shuile, &c.

SHULE AGRAH.

Oft I roved my garden bowers,
To gaze upon fast fading flowers,
And think upon past happy hours
    That's fled like summer's bloom.
  Shule, Shule, Shule arrah,
  Time can never end my woe,
  Since the lad of my heart did go,
    Gudhe tough, gudhe tough, slaun.

No more am I that blooming maid,
That used to rove the valley's shade;
My youth, my bloom, are both decayed,
    And every charm is gone.
      Shule, Shule, Shule, &c.

For now he's gone to other climes,
To seek one more pleasing to his mind;
But ah, the maid he left behind
    Shall love him best of all.
      Shule, Shule, Shule, &c.

His eyes were black, his coat was blue,
His hair was fair, his heart was true;
I wish in my heart I was with you,
    Gudhe tough, gudhe tough, slaun.
      Shule, Shule, Shule, &c.
The time can only ease my woe,
Since the lad of my heart from me did go.
    Uska dhe, uska dhe, mavourneen
      slaun.

I'll sell my rack, I'll sell my reel,
When my flax is out I'll sell my wheel,
To buy my love a sword and shield.
    Gudhe tough, gudhe tough, &c.

I wish I was in yonder hill,
It's there I'd sit and cry my fill,
That every tear would turn a mill.
    Gudhe tough, gudhe tough, slaun.
      Shule, Shule, Shule, &c.

Oft I've sat on my love's knee,
Many a fond story he told to me;
He said many things that ne'er will be.
    Gudhe tough, gudhe tough, &c.

I'll dye my petticoat, I'll dye it red,
That round the world I may beg my bread,
And then my parents would wish me dead.
    Gudhe tough, gudhe tough, slaun.
      Shule, Shule, Shule, &c.
Time can only ease my woe,
Since the lad of my heart from me did go.
    Uska dhe, Uska dhe, mavourneen
      slaun.

PAGE
107. *Go-thee-thu mavourneen slaun* = **farewell, my darling.**
    Shule agra = come, my love.

NOTES.

PAGE
108. *I sold my rock, I sold my reel.* "Rock" and "reel," two parts of an Irish spinning-wheel.

The Wild Geese = the Irish Jacobites who left their country for service in the French army when the cause of James II. was lost.

Mabouchal = my boy.

That every tear would turn a mill = "so that" every tear, &c.

109. *I'll dye my petticoat, &c.* Probably a red petticoat was the usual mark of a beggar in the time when this ballad was written.

Gragalmachree.

110. *Gra-gal-machree*, in plain English "fair love of my heart."

Put your comether = put your love spell, comether being a contraction of the words "come hither."

My song is founded on the following original, copied from a collection of old ballads in the Library of the Royal Irish Academy :—

At the foot of Newry mountain there runs a clear stream ;
Fain would I marry pretty Polly by name ;
She's slender in the waist, for young men to see,
And her name in plain Irish is Gragalmachree.

'Twas on a summer's morning, as I walked along,
Down by a green valley, I heard a fine song ;
'Twas a fair damsel, with her voice most clear,
Saying, how blest would I be if my darling was here.

I then drew near to a shade that was green,
Where the leaves grew about her and she scarce could be seen ;
And it was her whole cry, my darling come away,
For without your loving company no longer can I stay.

The moon it may darken and shew no light,
And the bright stars of heaven fall down quite ;
And the rocks may melt, and the mountains move
If ever I prove false to the fair one I love.

If I were an empress and had the care of a crown,
And had all the money that's for it laid down,
I would freely remit it to the boy that I love,
And my mind I'd resign to the great God above.

Like a sheet of white paper is her neck and breast,
She's slender in the waist and her hair is brown,
She's a pattern of virtue wherever she goes,
And her cheeks I compare to the red blushing rose.

NOTES.

The ships on the ocean may go without sails,
And the smallest of fishes may turn into whales,
And in the midst of the ocean may grow apple trees,
If ever I prove false to my Gragalmachree.

'Twas Pretty to be in Ballinderry.

112. Suggested by the stanza on p. 42 of Bunting's collection:—

> It's pretty to be in Ballinderry,
>   It's pretty to be in Aghalee,
>   It's prettier to be in bonny Ram's Island
>   Sitting under an ivy tree.
>   Ochone, &c.
> Oh! that I was in little Ram's Island,
> Oh! that I was with Phelimy Diamond.
> He would whistle and I would sing,
> Till we would make the whole island ring.

The scene of this ballad, as the names of the places mentioned in it will show, is laid on the shore of Loch Neagh.

My Bonny Cuckoo.

(*See* MUSICAL APPENDIX, p. 231.)

114. This ballad is based upon two stanzas to a song, "The Bonny Cuckoo," in Bunting's collection, which runs as follows:—

> My Bonny Cuckoo, I tell thee true,
> That through the groves I'll rove with you,
> I'll rove with you until the next Spring,
> And then my cuckoo shall sweetly sing,
> Cuckoo! cuckoo! until the next spring;
> And then my cuckoo shall sweetly sing.
>
> The Ash and the Hazel shall mourning say,
> My bonny cuckoo, don't go away;
> Don't go away, but tarry here,
> And make the season last all the year.

The Willow Tree.

116. But slightly altered from the following, which I found in the Library of the Royal Irish Academy:—

> Oh, take me to your arms, love, for keen the wind doth blow;
> Oh, take me to your arms, love, so bitter is my woe;
> She hears me not, she cares not, nor will she list to me,
> While here I lie, alone to die, beneath the willow tree.

260   *NOTES.*

PAGE

    My love has wealth and beauty, and I, alas! am poor;
    This ribband fair that bound her hair is all that's left to me.
    While here I lie, alone to die, beneath the willow tree.

    I once had gold and silver, and I thought e'en without end;
    I once had gold and silver, and I thought I had a friend;
    My wealth is lost, my friend is false, my love is stole from me,
    While here I lie, alone to die, beneath the willow tree.

For an interesting note upon the air of "The Willow Tree," see p. 75 of Dr. Joyce's "Ancient Irish Music," Gill and Co., 50, Upper Sackville Street, Dublin.

Jack the Jolly Ploughboy.

117. This poem is based upon the following verse, which will be found printed on p. 20 of Bunting's collection:—

    'Twas Jack the Jolly Plough-boy was ploughing in his land,
    Cried "Yough!" unto his horses, and boldly bid them stand.
    Then Jack sat down upon his plough, and thus began to sing,
    And Jack he sung his song so sweet he made the valleys ring.
           With his Too-ran-nan-nanty na,
           Sing Too-ran-nan-nanty na,
      Sing Too-ran-nan, Too-ran-nan, Too-ran-nan, Too-ran-nan,
           Too-ran-nan-nanty na.

118. The Golden Vale in Tipperary and Limerick.

Jenny.

119. Founded on the following ballad obtained by me in the Library of the Royal Irish Academy:—

        At dawn I rose with jocund glee,
           For joyful was the day,
        That could this blessing give to me,
           Now joy is fled away, Jenny.
        Nor flocks nor herds, nor store of gold,
           Nor house nor home have I;
        If beauty must be bought and sold,
           Alas! I cannot buy, Jenny.

        Yet I am rich, if thou art kind,
           So priz'd a smile from thee;
        True love alone our hearts shall bind,
           Thou'rt all the world to me, Jenny.
        Sweet, gentle maid, tho' patient, meek,
           My lily drops a tear,
        Ah! raise thy drooping head, and seek
           Soft peace and comfort here, Jenny.

The Fox Hunt.

PAGE
120. I am indebted to Dr. Joyce for the following broadsheet version of the ballad "Tally-ho! hark-a-way," the rollicking air to which will be well known to many of my readers, and on which, for I have not seen any other version of it, my lines are founded:—

TALLY HO! HARK AWAY.

It was on the first of March, in the year of thirty-three,
There was fun and recreation in our own country;
The King's County sportsmen, o'er hills, dales, and rocks,
Most nobly set out in the search of a fox.

CHORUS.

Tally ho! hark away! tally ho! hark away.
Tally ho! hark away! my boys, away, hark away!

When they started poor Reynard he fac'd to Tullamore,
Through Wicklow and Arklow, along the sea-shore,
They kept him in view the whole length of the way,
And closely pursued him through the streets of Roscrea.

When Reynard was started he faced down the hollow,
Where none but the huntsmen and hounds they could follow;
The gentlemen cried "Watch him," saying "What shall we do here?
If the hills and dales don't stop them he will cross to Kildare."

There were one hundred and twenty sportsmen went down to Ballyland,
From that to Blyboyne[1] and Ballycumminsland;
But Reynard, sly Reynard, arrived on that night,
And they said they would watch him until the daylight.

It was early next morning the hills they did appear,
With the echoes of the horn and the cry of the hounds;
But in spite of his action, his craft, and his skill,
He was taken by young Donohoe going down Moranze.

When Reynard was taken his wishes to fulfil,
He called for pen, ink, and paper, to write his last will,
And what he made mention of you'll find it is no blank,
For he gave them a cheque on the National Bank.

Hullahoo, an Irish equivalent for "Tally ho!"

---

[1] Broadsheet spelling for Ballyboyne.

The Fairy Branch.

PAGE
125. This poem is founded upon a prose tale, "How Cormac Mac Airt got his Branch," a literal translation of which Celtic tale will be found on p. 213 of "Transactions of the Ossianic Society for the Year 1855," Vol. III. But there is an older version in the Book of Ballymote.

Arch King of Erin, Ard Righ Erind; i.e., "The paramount King, or High King of Erin, who resided at Tara until the middle of the seventh century," p. 231., Vol. I., of "Manners and Customs of the Ancient Irish," by Professor O'Curry.

His Dun in Liathdrum = his Royal Fort in Tara.

126. *Cairbré* = Cairbre Liffeachair.
128. *That held the blackbirds hushed in Derrycarn.* These birds are rendered famous by Ossian.

129.   *His daily round*
      Of royal duty.

"There are now seven occupations in the law of a king: viz., Sunday, at ale drinking, for he is not a lawful Flaith who does not distribute ale every Sunday; Monday, at legislation, for the government of the tribe; Tuesday, at chess; Wednesday, seeing grey-hounds coursing; Thursday, at the pleasures of love; Friday, at horse-racing; Saturday, at judgment."—O'Curry, "Manners and Customs of the Ancient Irish."

Torque = the neck-torque or gorget of spirally twisted gold.
Fails = bracelets.

130. *The king's high Ollamh* = the Chief Justice of the Airecht Fodeisen or King's Court.

          Penalty
Exceeding great for satire.

"From the remotest time down to our own," writes Professor O'Curry, "the power of satire was dreaded in Erin, and the 'enecland' or penalty for it was serious."

The Brehon who rehearsed the Rann (or satire) = the inferior judge to the presiding Ollamh, one of the Brethem no Dobeir who sat in the King's Court. See p. 272, Vol. I., of O'Curry's "Manners and Customs of the Ancient Irish."

132. *Timpan*, a stringed instrument of music, but as to how it was played and what it was like we are left in doubt.

134. *Her yellow curls, clustering like rings of gold.*

The passage in the "Lay of Oisin on the Land of Youths," describing Niamh, has the following:—

> A gold ring was hanging down
> From each yellow curl of her golden hair.

136. *The hand-log* = a wooden knocker.

A royal hall. The description of Mananan's palace is based upon information on early Irish interiors to be found in Professor O'Curry's work.

137. *A great wood-ranging . . . boar.* The wild boar is very frequently alluded to in the Bardic Poems.

139. *Kieves* or *keeves* = tubs.

Mananan, the chief of the Dedannans, or Irish pagan deities, was a sea-god, and gave his name to the Isle of Man.

Beltane.

144. *Beltane* = May-day. My lines are a verse rendering of the following translation from a beautiful though obscure lyrical fragment attributed to Finn Mac Cumhiall, the traditionary leader of the Feni:—

May day, delightful time! how beautiful the color!
The blackbirds sing their full lay, would that Laighaig were here;
The cuckoos sing in constant strains, how welcome is the noble
Brilliance of the seasons ever; on the margin of the branchy woods
The summer suaill (swallows) skim the stream, the swift horses seek the pool,
The heath spreads out its long hair, the weak fair bog-down grows.
Sudden consternation attacks the signs, the planets in their courses running exert an influence:
The sea is lulled to rest, flowers cover the earth.

Mr. John O'Daly, as editor of the "Transactions of the Ossianic Society for 1856," thus writes of this poem: "The words of this fragment, which was considered to be the first composition of Finn, after having eaten the salmon of the Boyne, is very ancient and exceedingly obscure. The translation is only offered for the consideration of Irish scholars, for it is certain that the meaning of some of the lines is doubtful. The poem obviously wants some lines at the end, and Mr. Cleaver states that the remaining portion of the manuscript is so defaced as to render it totally illegible."

Patrick and Oisin.

PAGE
145. Oisin, the Irish Ossian, after several centuries' sojourn in Fairyland, returns to Erin, riding on a magic steed, only to find his heroic Finian comrades passed away from the land. By neglecting to keep his feet from Irish soil, as enjoined by the fairies, he suddenly shrinks from a stalwart champion into a decrepit old man, and becomes until death a discontented dependant of St. Patrick and his monks.

My poem is a translation of a few verses of a long Celtic poem, the "Dialogue of Oisin and Patrick," which will be found in the "Transactions of the Ossianic Society for 1856," and to which I gladly refer my readers, not only on account of its great poetical merits, but also because of its remarkable psychological interest.

Dord-Finn chorus = the Dord Fiansa, "which," writes Professor O'Curry, "I should take to be a species of military chorus or concert."

Letter Lee. This place is not yet identified.

Gleann-a-Sgail = the Glen of Scal.

146. *Derrycarn*, an oakwood in the county of Meath.

Glennamoo = the glen of victories.

The Ridge by the stream. Unidentified.

Tra-Rury = a loud surge in the Bay of Dundrum, co. Down.

Irrus = Erris, a barony in the north-west of Mayo.

The Suir. "The first, the gentle Shure, that making way
By sweet Clonmell, adorns rich Waterford."
*Spenser's "Fairy Queen," Bk. II.,
canto xi., verse 43.*

Cucullain's Lament over Ferdiah.

147. Ferdiah, chief of the Fir-bolgs, is tempted by the promise of great possessions and the hand of Fionavar, daughter of Queen Maev, whose whole army his best friend, Cucullain, the Champion of the Red Branch, is keeping at bay, to go out and do battle with the hero. Cucullain slays him after a fierce struggle, and thus laments over his corpse, taking in his hand the royal brooch which the Queen had given him. (Observe Cucullain and Ferdiah, though obliged to fight, were dear old friends) :—

> Alas! oh, golden brooch!
>   Oh, Ferdiah of the poets!
>   Oh, stout hero of slaughtering blows!
>   Valiant was thine arm.
>
> Thy yellow, flowing hair,
>   The curled, the beauteous jewel;
>   Thy soft, foliated girdle
>   Upon thy side till death.
>
> Delightful thy fellow-pupilship;
>   Beaming, noble eyes;
>   Thy shield with its golden rim;
>   Thy chess which was worth riches.
>
> Thy fall by my hand,
>   I feel it was not right.
>   It was not a friendly consummation.
>   Alas! O golden brooch, alas!

The whole of the story of Cucullain and Ferdiah is most eloquently and touchingly told in the first volume of "The History of Ireland," by Standish O'Grady; Sampson Low and Co., London.

The Song of the Fairy King.

148. "This Midir (the Fairy King), like the rest of his race, was an accomplished magician; and, in a short time after the marriage of Edain, he appeared in disguise at the palace of Tara. He asked to play a game at chess with the monarch Eochaidh Fedleach, and won the queen Edain as the stake." As he is about to carry off the queen, he thus addresses her:—

> "O *Befinn* (Fair Woman), will you come with me
> To a wonderful country which is mine,
> Where the people's hair is of golden hue,
> And their bodies the colour of virgin snow?
> There no grief or care is known;
> White are their teeth, black their eyelashes;
> Delight of the eye is the rank of our hosts,
> With the hue of the fox-glove on every cheek.
> Crimson are the flowers of every mead,
> Gracefully speckled as the blackbird's egg;
> Though beautiful to see be the plains of Innisfail,
> They are but commons compared to our great plains.
> Though intoxicating to you be the ale-drink of Innisfail,
> More intoxicating the ales of the great country;
> The only land to praise is the land of which I speak,
> Where no one ever dies of decrepit age.

> Soft sweet streams traverse the land ;
> The choicest of mead and wine ;
> Beautiful people without any blemish ;
> Love without sin, without wickedness.
> We can see the people upon all sides,
> But by no one can we be seen ;
> The cloud of Adam's transgression it is
> That prevents them from seeing us.
> O Woman ! should you come to my brave land,
> It is golden hair will be on your head ;
> Fresh pork, beer, new milk, and ale,
> You there shall have with me, O Béfinn !"

This remarkable story and poem are regarded by Professor O'Curry, from whose writings I have made the above extracts, as of great antiquity. The incident is most poetically worked out in prose by Mr. Standish O'Grady, in a chapter entitled "The Fairy Bride," in his "History of Ireland," Vol. I.

O'Curnan's Song.

150. To my friend, Dr. Joyce, I am indebted for the following brief sketch (supplied to him by Mr. John Fleming, of Rathgormack, in the county Waterford) of one of our most remarkable Irish peasant poets, O'Curnan :—

Poor O'Curnan's story was tragical enough. Hired by a farmer in Modeligo, who had but one child, a little girl, O'Curnan was given to understand that on her coming to a marriageable age, her hand and the farm together would be bestowed upon him, provided he served faithfully until then. He served seven years, it is said, and, like the patriarch of old, was cheated. Being sent to Cork to sell some loads of corn and buy the wedding dress, etc., the young woman, during his absence, was married to another man who had a fortune. O'Curnan travelled day and night, but a long journey a century ago could not be got over in a hurry. As he approached the home of his betrothed early in the morning, he was met by the wedding party going to their respective homes after the night, and it is said that some of them made him the butt of their ridicule. Entering the house, and learning how matters stood, he threw into the fire the "favours" he had brought from Cork, as well as his own wedding clothes, and for ever after roamed over the country a madman—but with his poetical powers intact—and always engaged in singing his own misfortunes and the cruelty of his Mary. O'Curnan's story was known to every man and woman in the county of Waterford fifty years ago, and there are persons still living who have seen him.

Dr. Joyce has also furnished me with the subjoined literal translation of O'Curnan's most popular love lyric, versified by me in the same measure as the original under the above title:—

O Mary, sweet and fair, who left this sigh in the midst of my heart,
   That the Island of Fōdla would not heal,
I would swear by my hand, hadst thou understood my case,
   That thou would'st not let me die without relief.
I do not take an ounce of food, I do not sleep when I lie down,
   There is no liveliness nor strength in me, but I am like a small shadow;
And unless I find time and opportunity to speak with the love of my innermost heart,
   I shall not be alive in a quarter nor in a month.

No one alive knows my trouble, or how to cure it,
   Except only the maiden who has left me heart-sick;
My cure is not to be found in sea or on strand, nor in herb nor in skill of hand;
   My cure is nowhere to be found except with the Flower of Youthfulness!
I know not the cuckoo from the hen, I know not heat from cold,
   I do not at any time recognise my friends;
I know not night from day—but well would my heart know its True-love,
   If she would only come in time, and save me!

Save me, dear love, save me! give me one sweet kiss from thy mouth,
   And lift me back again to thee from death;
Or bespeak for me a narrow bed, in a close deal coffin,
   In the company of the chafer and his kindred.
My life is not life, but death; by voice is not voice, but mere breath;
   I have no colour, no life, no health;
But I am tearful, sad, feeble, without music, without amusement, without vigour,
   In hard slavery and pain for love of thee!

150. *Mary bawn asthore* = fair-haired Mary, my treasure.
   The Isle of Fōdla = Ireland.

Caoine.

(See Musical Appendix, p. 234.)

152. This *Caoine, keen* or lamentation, is written to the music of the "Ulster Goll," which will be found at length in Bunting's collection. It is a verse translation or adaptation from one of

Crofton Croker's Irish Keens, which I find thus quoted at p. 326 of Vol. I. of "Hayes' Ballads of Ireland:"

> "Cold and silent is thy bed. Damp is the blessed dew of night; but the sun will bring warmth and heat in the morning, and dry up the dew. But thy heart cannot feel heat from the morning sun: no more will the print of your footsteps be seen in the morning dew, on the mountains of Ivera, where you have so often hunted the fox and the hare, ever foremost amongst young men. Cold and silent is now thy bed.
>
> "My sunshine you were. I loved you better than the sun itself; and when I see the sun going down in the west, I think of my boy and of my black night of sorrow. Like the rising sun, he had a red glow on his cheek. He was as bright as the sun at midday; but a dark storm came on, and my sunshine was lost to me for ever. My sunshine will never again come back. No! my boy cannot return. Cold and silent is his bed." . . .

Snow Stains.

164. An American poem, "Beautiful Snow," has a good deal in common with these lines. I had better, therefore, say that I have never seen that poem, and that it was not repeated to me until five years after my own was written.

A Song of the Seasons.

166. Suggested by one of Barry Cornwall's lyrics, which is in the same measure, and which devotes a stanza to each of the four seasons.

The Rejected Lover.

(*See* MUSICAL APPENDIX, p. 235.)

171. Suggested by these few lines in Bunting's collection to the air of "The Rejected Lover:"

> "Her hair was like the beaten gold,
>   Or like the spider's spinning;
> It was in her you might behold
>   My joys and woes beginning."

Ambrose and Una.

176. This is a literal verse rendering of a prose translation of the Danish ballad, "Aäge and Elsé," furnished me by Mr. Peter Toft.

Companions.

PAGE
198. This song, under the title of "The Two Friends" has been set to music by Mr. Joseph Robinson, and is published by Cramer, Wood, and Co., Westmorland Street, Dublin.

Good Night.

(*See* MUSICAL APPENDIX, p. 239.)

199. Suggested by and written to an air in Petrie's collection entitled, "Good Night, and Joy be with you all."

INDEX.

SONGS AND BALLADS :—

	PAGE
The Little Red Lark	3
Love's Wishes	5
I Once Loved a Boy	6
The Banks of the Daisies	7
Herring is King	9
Hush Song	12
The Foggy Dew	14
The Confession	16
The Girl I left behind me	18
Eva Tuohill	20
'Tis I can weave Woollen and Linen	22
Maureen, Maureen	23
When I rose in the Morning	25
The Mill Song	27
'Tis a pity I can't see my love	30
With the North	32
Nancy, the Pride of the West	35
Jenny, I'm not Jesting	37
The Hour we Parted	40
The Smith's Song	43
Mo Muirnin Dhu	45
Pleraca	47
Song of the Ghost	50
Colleen Oge Asthore	53
The Flight of the Earls	56
Kitty Bhan	58
The White Blossom 's off the Bog	59
With Fluttering Joy	60
A Sailor loved a Farmer's Daughter	61
The Reaper's Revenge	63
The Blue, Blue Smoke	65

RUSTIC POEMS :—

Father O'Flynn	71
Molleen Oge	74
Two Irish Idylls	76

INDEX.

Rustic Poems *(continued):*—

	PAGE
Fan Fitzgerl	79
Bat of the Bridge	81
The Light in the Snow	87
What is Life widout a Wife?	90
The Wreck of the Aideen	93
The Handsome Witch	95
Saving the Turf	98
Loobeen	99
The Black '46	102

Anglo-Irish Ballads:—

Shuile Agra	107
Gragalmachree	110
'Twas pretty to be in Ballinderry	112
My Bonny Cuckoo	114
The Willow Tree	116
Jack the Jolly Ploughboy	117
Jenny	119
The Fox Hunt	120

From the Celtic:—

The Fairy Branch	125
Beltane	144
Patrick and Oisin	145
Cucullain's Lament over Ferdiah	147
The Song of the Fairy King	148
O'Curnan's Song	150
Caoine	152

Songs and Sketches:—

Song	155
From the Red Rose	157
O Branch of Fragrant Blossom	158
One Loving Smile	159
Snow Drift	160
Shamrock Leaves	163
Snow Stains	164
A Song of the Seasons	166
Maureen	168
Spring's Secrets	169
The Rejected Lover	171
The Beautiful Bay	173
Ambrose and Una	176
Orpheus to Pluto	181
Song: To E. P.	185

INDEX.

SONGS AND SKETCHES *(continued)* :—

	PAGE
Choosing a Profession	188
Myrtilla	190
Love's Surprise	191
Amœbæan	193
Love's Song	196
Companions	198
Good Night	199

MUSIC :—

The Little Red Lark	203
Love's Wishes	204
I Once Loved a Boy	205
Hush Song	206
The Foggy Dew	207
The Confession	208
Maureen, Maureen	210
When I rose in the Morning	212
'Tis a pity I can't see my love	213
With the North	214
Jenny, I'm not Jesting	216
The Hour we Parted	218
The Smith's Song	219
Pleraca	220
Song of the Ghost	222
Colleen Oge Asthore	223
The Flight of the Earls	224
A Sailor loved a Farmer's Daughter	225
Father O'Flynn	227
'Twas pretty to be in Ballinderry	229
My Bonny Cuckoo	231
Jack the Jolly Ploughboy	232
Caoine	234
The Rejected Lover	235
Irish Spinning Wheel Song	236
Irish Lullaby	238
Good Night	239

NOTES :—

The Little Red Lark	243
Love's Wishes	243
I Once Loved a Boy	243
The Banks of the Daisies	244
Herring is King	244
Hush Song	244
The Foggy Dew	245
The Confession	245

S

NOTES (continued):—

	PAGE
The Girl I left behind me	245
Eva Tuohill	245
'Tis I can weave Woollen and Linen	246
Maureen, Maureen	246
When I rose in the Morning	246
The Mill Song	246
'Tis a pity I can't see my love	246
With the North	246
Nancy, the Pride of the West	247
Jenny, I'm not Jesting	247
The Hour we Parted	247
The Smith's Song	247
Mo Muirnin Dhu	248
Pleraca	248
Song of the Ghost	249
Colleen Oge Asthore	249
The Flight of the Earls	250
Kitty Bhan	251
The White Blossom's off the Bog	251
With Fluttering Joy	251
A Sailor loved a Farmer's Daughter	252
The Reaper's Revenge	252
The Blue, Blue Smoke	252
Father O'Flynn	253
Molleen Oge	253
Two Irish Idylls	253
Fan Fitzgerl	253
Bat of the Bridge	253
The Light in the Snow	254
What is Life widout a Wife?	254
The Wreck of the Aideen	254
The Handsome Witch	254
Saving the Turf	255
Loobeen	255
The Black '46	256
Shuile Agra	256
Gragalmachree	258
'Twas pretty to be in Ballinderry	259
My Bonny Cuckoo	259
The Willow Tree	259
Jack the Jolly Ploughboy	260
Jenny	260
The Fox Hunt	261
The Fairy Branch	262
Beltane	263
Patrick and Oisin	264
Cucullain's Lament over Ferdiah	264

NOTES *(continued)*:—

	PAGE
The Song of the Fairy King	265
O'Curnan's Song	266
Caoine	267
Snow Stains	268
A Song of the Seasons	268
The Rejected Lover	268
Ambrose and Una	268
Companions	269
Good Night	269

𝕿𝖍𝖊 𝕰𝖓𝖉.

A. IRELAND AND CO., PRINTERS, PALL MALL, MANCHESTER.

CORRIGENDA.

P. 3. Supply a comma at the end of line 13.
P. 13. Convert the comma at the end of line 11 into a full stop.
P. 20. Transfer comma from end of line 18 to end of line 17.
Pp. 45, 46. For "moireen" read "muirnin."
P. 77. Strike out comma at end of line 7.
P. 93. Cancel comma before "Aideen."
P. 103, line 4. For "right" read "night."
,, lines 10, 12. For "dawn" read "shade," and for "slan" "spade."
Pp. 107-109. For "Gotheen" read "Go-thee-thu."
P. 109. Supply comma at end of line 16.
P. 121, line 8. For "Blyboyne" read "Ballyboyne."
P. 129, line 13. Before "smote" supply "wildly."
P. 130, line 3. For "hundred-battled" read "hundred-fighter."

www.ingramcontent.com/pod-product-compliance
Lightning Source LLC
Chambersburg PA
CBHW031938230426
43672CB00010B/1965